Hooked?

Young People; Drugs & Alcohol

Yvonne Ward

ATTIC PRESS
DUBLIN

Contents

Chapter One

Some Alcohol and Drug-Users

It was late. In fact it was very late indeed. The whole house was in darkness, the blinds pulled and the doors locked. Only the family cat was awake and witnessed the way John struggled with the key. He was trying very hard to be quiet. He didn't want his mum and dad to wake; he didn't want to have to answer any questions; he didn't want to talk to anyone at all. The ginger cat miaowed encouragingly at John. With luck she might manage a bed in the warm house for a change.

Leaning against the door for support, John fumbled and prodded with the key. It still wouldn't go into the lock. He held the key close to his eyes, blinked and tried again. Ginger rubbed insistently against his leg and he gave her a kick. Mumbling obscenities to himself John made a desperate jab at the Yale lock and the door finally burst open.

He was, literally, nearly legless drunk. It had been quite an evening, an evening that seemed a blurry dream to him as he slowly levered himself up the stairs. He hoped his stomach was empty. He had already emptied it several times on the path during the walk home. As he fell into bed and into a deeply unconscious sleep, his last thought was, 'Gosh! that was great!'

Two doors away, Tom's bed was still empty. He wouldn't be back tonight, and this was not the first occasion. Exam results weren't necessary to give Tom an excuse to go on the tear. Tom's mother lay awake and tearful beside her husband. He had double-locked the front door when it reached 2.30 a.m. He was sick and tired of the constant fighting, arguing and breaking of deadlines. 'He can go sleep wherever the hell he likes,' he shouted in response to her entreaties about Tom and his safety. 'He can hardly justify being out to celebrate the exam results. He failed every subject but one, the lazy, feckless good-for-nothing.'

At the back of it all, Val was just as worried and desperate

1

as his wife. Tom was his only son and there had always been an easy, warm rapport between them. Now it seemed as if that had all vanished. Nothing appeared to get through to him these days. He was quiet around the house, either locked in his room listening to loud rhythmic music or slouched in various chairs gazing into the mid-distance. Trying to talk to him seemed impossible. At times he looked at you and after several minutes said, 'Uh?' or 'What?' as if he had been on another planet. Or he said, 'Yeah, yeah' and then got up and switched on the music video channel on the television or walked out of the room.

Val blamed it all on the gang of lads Tom was hanging around with. Tom was out of the house most nights until late. On a couple of occasions he hadn't come home until morning. The first time they had rung the police and all the local hospitals and any of Tom's friends that they knew about. He had turned up the next day looking dishevelled, pale and as if he hadn't slept in a week. Despite threats, shouting and pleading he and Sheila had not been made any the wiser about his whereabouts. Tom had become increasingly uninterested in his appearance, rarely washing and certainly never tidying up after him. They didn't often open his bedroom door—the whiff was so strong and the disorder was so apparent. Sheila wouldn't confess it to Val but she had regularly tried to sort the room out. However Tom disapproved so loudly and in such a determined manner that she had given up.

She didn't know how to handle Tom. It was like living with a lodger; worse, it was like living with a ill-mannered uninterested stranger. A year before Tom had been suspended from school. The teachers had said he was sleeping in class, playing truant and behaving rudely towards the staff. His grades had dropped, though they hadn't been too great at the best of times. Seemingly he had not been doing his homework either. Val and Sheila were angry with the school as they had not realised up to then that Tom's performance had deteriorated so much. They had hoped he was just going through the normal teenage blues, that this was what was happening in every other house and that it was just a phase he would grow out of.

According to Tom he didn't like school, was bored to death

of geography, history, French and religious studies. He wanted to leave school, get a job, maybe work with his dad. Even at that stage Val had blamed it all on Tom's buddies, the bad influences who were twisting Tom's mind. They grounded him indefinitely and entered into negotiations with the school to get him back. Reluctantly, without any interest, Tom agreed to attend school regularly, pay attention and do his homework. On this basis, the school was prepared to let him prepare for his exams.

Sheila and Val had been aware that Tom continued to do the minimum. His homework seemed to consist of shutting himself into the bedroom and playing his music at a deafening volume. Talking to other parents, Sheila learned that most of the teenagers played music while doing homework; she was relieved. Her relief was short-lived. Tom's exam results had borne out their ill-concealed fears. 'Where is he?' 'What is he doing?' 'Who is he with?' 'He is just 16 years old and he is throwing away his future.' 'What can we do?'

Even at this stage neither Val nor Sheila connected Tom's behaviour with drugs or alcohol.

Alice had also had a great evening. She drank most weekends, and though it had been an extra-special evening (after all she had got five honours and four passes in her Junior Cert), she had not had any more to drink than the three glasses of cider she normally had. Well, normally she drank two cans, in a friend's house rather than at a disco. She did not approve of drugs and had steadfastly refused the joints her friend Anna and Anna's mates had offered her. The idea of drugs terrified her; she did not like the idea of losing control or maybe going off her head. Everyone said that a bit of blow or hash, didn't do you any harm. They constantly offered her a pull, saying: 'Want some? You don't know what you're missing; it won't make you sick or anything! Come on—it'll make you feel great.'

They all knew she smoked cigarettes and thought she was mad because she wouldn't smoke a joint. 'Cigarettes are one thing,' she thought, 'but I'm not going to pollute my body with drugs. I'll just stick to a few drinks and a few cigarettes.' Alice was very conscious of pollution; she had recently become a vegetarian. She did not see alcohol or tobacco as pollutants or even drugs, or if she did, she pushed the thought quickly and firmly out of her head!

Most of Alice's circle of friends thought along similar lines. A few drinks were one thing but not blow [hash]. The lads seemed to be big into the hash but the girls stuck mostly to having a drink. 'Are you going drinking tonight?' was the regular question as they huddled along the wall at the back of the science labs having their breaktime puff. Smoking wasn't permitted on the school grounds but everyone managed it. Some of the lads were known to be smoking hash. They didn't seem to care. 'Are we going to the football pitch?'

'No, Jean's parents are going out. She says we can go there.'

This was how Alice had served her apprenticeship to alcohol, along with most of the other girls in her year who drank. They would meet together, girls only, and sample the selection at certain houses where booze was readily available. In some houses there was such a generous supply that their parents didn't seem to notice the cans of beer or cider disappearing. Granted it would be a half-dozen here, two or three there, but Alice was amazed that nothing was said. Her own parents were more vigilant, and anyway they never had alcohol in the house. Usually there was a mix of ages. Some of the girls had older sisters and the sisters and their mates would be part of the groups for drinking. When there wasn't a house available they would meet up on the pitch or the field down the road. There might be only two or three of them at a time, sometimes more. The older girls would go along to the local off-licence for them or at times they got their boyfriends to buy cans for them—the lads were usually older.

In Alice's experience there was no problem getting drink. Sometimes someone snitched it from home or, if they were stuck, some of the bolder girls would go along and ask someone going into the off-licence to buy them some. There never seemed to be any difficulty in getting men, women or older teenagers to buy alcohol for them. Even Alice was amazed that they never seemed to question their age. Indeed it was well known that there was a supermarket nearby that sold alcohol to anyone who asked for it, under-age or not. The furthest a drink would ever be was a long walk away.

4

Most of the girls stuck to this pattern, with the occasional foray into social occasions such as tonight. They would be on their guard in these situations. Alice herself felt quite sickened by what she considered the way the lads 'groped' around you if they thought you had been drinking. They seemed to think you were asking for it if you looked any way drunk. She always made sure she didn't lose control of the situation.

She wished the same thing could be said for her friend Anna. She worried a lot about Anna. Anna was two years older than she and had always looked out for her. Their mothers were friends and she guessed she had known Anna all of her life. Anna was tall and dark and to Alice the prettiest girl in the whole neighbourhood. Not only that but she was very clever. She seemed to be good at everything. She was always on top in her class, walked through exams and was brilliant on the piano. Her parents wanted her to succeed and had been nurturing her musical talents since she was a little girl. She even had a baby grand in her back room. You couldn't move or walk around it.

Anna was her parents' pride and joy but Alice reckoned it would drive her mad if her mum was constantly counting up her hours of piano practice and asking her to play for this one and that one. Anna didn't say much about it but Alice reckoned that it was something Anna didn't like either. Recently Anna had started hanging around with Chris, the local macho man. Chris was good-looking and popular in a dangerous sort of way. A lot of the girls fancied him from afar. He always seemed so confident, so sure of how he was coming across to everyone. Alice was frightened for Anna, because Chris was trouble with a capital 'T'. Even she knew that. Chris acted as if he didn't care what teachers said. He never seemed to pay any attention to anyone. He had failed all his exams and Alice knew this because everyone knew it. Chris was quite charming when he wanted to be and never caused trouble in school. He had a gorgeous grin and was polite to teachers and pupils alike. But at weekends when he was spaced out it was a different matter.

He had a motorbike and she had seen him herself trying to drive it when he was barely able to walk. He had been staggering around outside the shopping centre and then he hopped on the bike and tried to start it with the lock still on.

The bike reared and jumped, and he was lucky he hadn't got killed or burned or something. The other lads just laughed their heads off. Chris roared and screamed and started fighting with them.

Now Anna was spending time with him. Everyone knew he never stayed long with any girl. He changed girls more often than he changed his everyday uniform of black jeans, T-shirt and leather jacket. Tonight Anna had been with Alice and a couple of their friends at the beginning of the night but the minute Tessa and her cronies arrived, Anna had gravitated towards them. Tessa's boyfriend Patrick was always with Chris. Patrick was the school drug dealer. No matter how much or what kind you wanted, they said, all you had to do was place an order. Certainly he was the source of hash and micro-dots of acid for a lot of people. Again, Alice wondered why the teachers didn't know. They couldn't know, could they? Of course, maybe no one had told them. After all, Patrick was one of the school fixtures and she hadn't heard anyone ever getting too worked up about it. She had never thought too much about it until now. Not until Anna began to get involved with Patrick, Chris and their circle.

Tessa was in Alice's class. She was a nice looking girl. She got on all right in school, never top of the class, but never bottom either. Tessa didn't seem to stand out from the crowd; she blended in, did all the expected things. Alice had been astounded when Tessa began to boast about her boyfriend, the drug dealer. She seemed really proud of it, and proud not only of Patrick the dealer, but also of the fact that she used drugs also. Alice was shocked to learn that Tessa regularly used not only hash but speed and acid. 'It was something else,' Tessa said, and proceeded to describe the long trips she had on acid. 'Up to eight hours,' she said, 'and my mother didn't even guess. The colours, the feelings, the thoughts, I can't describe it; it was great! I knew what I was doing and then I could pretend to act normally if anyone was around.'

Alice didn't know what to make of all that. Was Tessa telling the truth? Did she take drugs? Had the trip really lasted for eight hours? Could you take drugs and not be harmed by them? Alice was very confused about all this. She thought that if she took drugs she would be ashamed and certainly wouldn't be boasting about it.

6

Meanwhile, tonight, as she lay in her bed and reflected on the evening, she hoped that Anna was OK. Her parents and Anna's parents had made arrangements for them to be picked up from the disco. Anna's parents always made sure they knew where she was and they would come along and drive her home. They still treated her exactly the same as Alice's parents treated her, despite the age difference. Tonight, though, Anna had gone off with Chris and his mates. She had had a good few drinks and Alice had known from the distinctive perfume that it wasn't a cigarette she had been smoking when she came over and whispered to Alice, 'Tell your parents I'm making my own way home. I'll be all right, don't worry!' Before Alice could agree, question or dispute it with her, Anna was gone. She had looked really happy, Alice reflected. Her eyes were bright, her cheeks were pink and she seemed excited. Alice sighed and turned over in her bed towards her favourite teddy bear.

This is a glimpse into the world of some young people. They could be any teenagers; they could be your pupils, your friend's children, your own children; they could be you. The reality is that drugs or mood-altering chemicals are one of the many issues that young people have to negotiate in their exciting and hazardous journey towards maturity. Another reality is that most of the adults around them find this journey just as puzzling and confusing as they do and, far from being confident role models and mentors, they are often only fellow travellers.

The passage from physical childhood into physical adulthood can take approximately eight to ten years, from about the age of eight to eighteen. These years encompass not only the process of physical development but also sexual development, emotional development, the development of independence and autonomy—a 'sense of self'.

In order to discover who they are or who they want to be, young people need to explore, challenge themselves and their ideas, attitudes and patterns of behaviour, to question and criticise ways of life. The years from childhood through adolescence to adulthood are about opening doors, avenues for growth and development. This also involves closing doors, leaving things behind.

One of the doors all teenagers open is the door that leads to chemical dependency. This does not mean that all young people become chemically dependent or addicted. But some (and evidence shows that it is an increasing number), do. The reality is that most if not all young people experiment. After all, once a young person sees a door, it is part of his or her nature to open it. This is because part of adolescence, part of the task of growing up, is to explore, experiment.

Mood-altering chemicals involve two major issues, pleasure and danger. Young people readily embrace pleasure and though they are sometimes concerned about danger, more readily deny and ignore it.

These are some of the questions young people and adults alike ask about mood-altering chemicals:

How much is too much?
Are all chemicals dangerous?
Why do some people become addicted?
Can it happen to me?
Why did it happen to me or my child?

The important issues are the same for all young people as they are for John, Tom, Alice, Anna and Chris and Patrick. When do they pass the point of no return? Is it safe to experiment as they are experimenting? When should they or their parents become concerned? How do they or their parents know if the changes in their attitudes, behaviour, appearance are due to personal choice and experimentation or to an unhealthy relationship with mood-altering chemicals, i.e. alcohol or drugs? To put it more simply, what is normal and healthy for an adolescent and what is unhealthy?

Mood-altering chemicals are part of culture and environment. They range from coffee, tea and over-the-counter drugs such as aspirin and paracetamol to prescribed drugs such as anti-histamines, sleeping tablets, tranquillisers; to household products such as aerosols, gas, petrol, glue; to legal drugs like alcohol and tobacco; to illegal drugs like hash, marijuana, acid (LSD), cocaine and heroin.

From an early age our children are exposed to some of these chemicals—in adolescence they encounter more of the illegal chemicals. Also in adolescence, or even before, it becomes possible to experiment, to try out a wider range of drugs. What we need to ensure is that young people have been given the degree of education, protection, attention, love and support that:

- Allows them to recognise when they are being hurt
- Teaches the hope of good feelings other than from chemicals
- Instils a belief in themselves and their own worth
- Gives the right to say yes or no for themselves
- Develops the ability to talk about their inner feelings

Young people need warm, loving, supportive relationships in their lives in order that they have these tools which will equip them to deal with the obstacles on the road to healthy, contented maturity. Dependency on mood-altering chemicals such as alcohol or other drugs can halt a young person's development. Unfortunately a relationship with drugs may itself be an attempt to cope with the tasks and trials of the path through adolescence.

Chapter Two

Delusions, Myths and Misguided Beliefs

Monday morning dawned bright and crisp. A typical autumn morning.

As the teenagers drifted towards school, many of them gathered in corners at the end of roads or by a convenient group of trees. They were having a quick drag of a cigarette before they reached the college grounds. Sam spluttered and coughed as he slowly made his way down the avenue. He was fourteen but he had a smoker's cough as good as any forty-year-old's. He had the stub of a smoke between his fingers and he sucked on it through clenched teeth as he shouldered his schoolbag and moved towards the school.

Sam looked at least a year younger than he was. He was blessed with Peter Pan looks which would benefit him greatly in years to come but which were a heavy cross to bear at present. He was the butt of many a joke and his nickname 'Babyface' was one which he struggled to rebut by his behaviour around the school and streets. He resorted to bullying, bragging and swaggering in an attempt to look older than his age or at least to gain respect as more than just a 'mammy's boy'. Sam was pretty much a loner, not gifted with repartee or ready wit. He had failed miserably in the social skills stakes and had no close friends. He hung around the edges of the gangs, trying desperately to fit in. This morning as he waited for the form teacher to arrive he boasted to the lad beside him, 'I went drinking this weekend.' As on every other Monday morning the lad beside him made no comment.

In truth no one believed Sam. He was known as someone who wanted to be the 'big fella' and who would say anything to impress. The other teenagers in his class would have been surprised to know that Sam had indeed gone drinking that weekend.

He lived in an adjoining district, about one and a half miles from the school. His family had moved house since he enrolled in the school, making Sam an outsider in yet another way. He was now an outsider in school, not from the local area, and an outsider at home, not from the local school. On Friday nights his home area had its youth club disco. This Friday night Sam had managed to get in with a crowd of older fellows who were going drinking before the disco. He had already taken two cans of beer from home and the lads had bought large flagons of cider. He had drunk as much as any of the others and had only the dimmest memory of going from the alley at the side of the estate towards the youth club.

Passing motorists had the alarming experience of trying to avoid Sam as he staggered across the busy roadway, shouting to no one in particular, talking to the cars as they passed, clutching a can in his hand. By some miracle he managed this hazardous journey safely several times, as he didn't seem to know where he was or where he wanted to be and crossed back and forth through the traffic as if he was playing a game. Sam thought he had chatted up a girl. The reality was that he spoke to one girl, leaned against her shoulder and fell flat on his back, beer-can still held aloft. She ignored him totally and walked on, chatting to her girlfriends.

People paid only passing attention to Sam as he stumbled along, obviously totally drunk. Occupants of cars turned their heads and stared. Mothers thought of their own early adolescent children and with relief dismissed the possibility that their children would ever be in that state. Some wondered if they should do anything and whether Sam's parents knew the state he was in. Others thought about him less kindly: one man opened his window and yelled furiously at Sam as he lurched between the cars. No one did anything. Finally Sam moved away from the road into a laneway and disappeared from view. He never made it to the disco. He ended up passing out at the back of the hall and waking up when an older lad shook his shoulder vigorously. 'Get up, the disco's over; you'd better get home.' No one at home found out about Sam's drinking episode. His parents were at a friend's house and his elder sister was not back from her night out. Nobody knew about Sam's drinking on other occasions either.

Not many in his class drank. Nearly all of them had experimented, though. Many of this bunch of fourteen-year-olds smoked occasionally, with a smaller group of about a dozen smoking constantly. There were more girls in this group. They had had all the usual lectures and talks but they did not think the danger applied to them. That all seemed too far away. They had plenty of time before anything they did caused them damage or harm. At least that was how the reasoning went. Meanwhile they enjoyed the high, the excitement of playing with danger, of fooling their parents, of rebelling against 'the rules'.

Jane felt more grown up, more independent, more of a woman of the world when she smoked. She had started in first year. The first morning at break, another girl had offered her a drag from her cigarette. Jane had felt a sense of belonging, even a sense of having arrived, in sharing that cigarette. It had been a gradual but definite progression from that to buying her own packet of cigarettes to share. Smoking meant more than just smoking to Jane. It had helped her fit in, to feel that she could be the same as the hundreds of other people at secondary school who seemed to her more confident, sophisticated and worldlywise than she could ever be. It helped her to cross the bridge from primary school to secondary school or so she thought.

There were other advantages to smoking, she found out. Lads would come and talk to her when they saw her smoking and they'd sometimes ask for a cigarette. It was a point of contact not only with lads in her own year but also with lads from the higher classes. She had something to share with them, something to do with them, and Jane found that smoking helped make possible a relationship with boys. She had begun to take the odd can of beer from the older lads when they were hanging out at the local park. She had hated the taste initially but enjoyed the sense of belonging to this relaxed group. Jane had matured physically at quite an early age. Her well developed figure had always seemed different, conspicuous even, among her still childlike friends. She also found herself more interested in boys and their attentions, or lack of them, than her friends were. Now she was fourteen they were catching up physically but she believed herself to be much more grown-up, more sophisticated than they were. Her illusions of maturity were based primarily on her relationship with tobacco and alcohol.

One aspect of her supposed popularity and sense of belonging which had escaped Jane's awareness was how she was viewed by other teenagers, particularly the boys she was drinking with. The lads thought of her as easy, available, even though in reality Jane was still a virgin and had no conscious intentions of doing anything more than the messing and clowning she got up to with the lads on their nights out. Their awareness of her intoxication fuelled their fantasy of her availability and lack of boundaries. The girls in her year thought of her as 'slutty', their term for other girls they believed to be sexually active. In part this was due to envy, when they saw her regularly in conversation with different lads during the break times in school, sharing furtive cigarettes at the far end of the yard. In part they viewed Jane in this way because they all knew that the girls who drank were more likely to have experimented sexually, intentionally or otherwise. They knew this from experience, from the girls who ended up pregnant or who boasted about their adventures. These girls, like Jane, had thought themselves more daring and cool than their friends or schoolmates who remained sober.

This Monday morning the buzz around the school was all about the excitements of the weekend. Stories and rumours abounded. Examination results were quoted and compared, along with accounts of the weekend celebrations. 'Did you hear about Keith? He drank a bottle of vodka as well as a few pints and he caused a riot in the pub. His girlfriend got her exam results and he went out with the crowd from her year. He thought another guy was paying her too much attention and he went crazy, broke up the place!' 'James Smith has a black eye.' 'We had the most fantastic time!' 'Mary got off with Mick at long last'. 'I walked Joan home from the disco. Wow! can she kiss!' 'Tom didn't go home at all on Friday night; his parents are threatening to keep him locked in all the time'. 'I went drinking on Saturday night'. 'Hash! That's only chickenfeed. I tried Ecstasy at the weekend. I went to a rave in town with my cousins. It was brilliant! I danced all night. It was the best ever.'

Alice met Anna on the corridors between classes. 'Well? How did it go?' she asked but Anna rushed by her, mumbling something about later. Alice watched her retreat down the hallway and realised she had a sinking feeling in the pit of her stomach. 'Oh dear, I hope she's OK.' Meanwhile Anna moved quickly towards her English class, hoping that no one else would stop her. Her luck was not in. Tessa was standing outside the English classroom door. 'Are you all right?' she whispered. 'Of course I'm all right,' Anna replied. 'I had a great night on Friday night but my mum and dad are really mad at me. I'm not allowed out for three weeks. I think I'll go mad if I have to stay in. Have you any blow?' [hash] 'I'll see you later. I'll meet you in the toilets, Anna,' Tessa responded. 'Are you sure you're all right?'

Anna would not have admitted it for the world but she was not OK. She could remember little of what had happened on the Friday night after they had left the disco. She had been drinking and smoking hash, and then just before they had left she had taken a couple of the tablets one of the lads offered her. She wasn't too sure what they were but the others had been taking them and she hadn't wanted to look stupid. At that point she hadn't cared anyway. She had been too high, she remembered, to worry about anything. She only had a vague memory of banging on the front door at home. She didn't know how she'd got there or even where she had been. Her mother had been ragging at her non-stop ever since. It was even a relief to get out to school this morning.

Keith was also keeping a low profile this morning. He had smoked a couple of joints already but he was on the look-out for Patrick for some better gear [drugs]. Not that many people would remark on his quietness because Keith was always quiet and retiring. This was why the occurrence on Friday night was making such a stir. James was parading his black eye like a badge of courage. Clare wasn't speaking to Keith but he knew that would wear off. At least he had Clare. She was the person he relied on. He had few friends. The truth was he had drugging companions rather than friends. He was deep into drugs and he was just about coping. Friday night had been a mistake, he reckoned. It was a big mistake to go drinking with the others. Keith's usual pattern when drinking was to stay on his own. When he drank, he drank to get drunk. All the talk just got in his way. Nowadays he preferred hash and acid. He felt more in control with them. He didn't need anyone around then.

Keith had been drinking for five years now. From the word go he loved alcohol. He loved the high, the blur it gave to the world; he just loved to get drunk. He is a quiet boy, bright at school, but a loner and introvert. He kept to himself, rarely voiced an opinion, never talked about his feelings. He was a middle child in his family, with an older brother and sister and two younger brothers. When he was eleven his parents had separated. He rarely saw his dad except at Christmas, Easter and for a few weekends during the summer. He lived down the country and had now got a second family, one little girl by his new wife. Keith did not think of this child as his sister. He didn't like to think at all about his father or his new wife.

Keith's mother was a quiet nervous woman. She looked old before her time, worn down by the pressures and worries of working and raising five children single-handed. The fact that Keith was rarely at home, had become more and more withdrawn, was not a worry to her. In many ways she saw this as a blessing. He was the child she didn't have to worry about the one who caused her no problems. He didn't demand attention and time from her as the others did. To her, Keith was getting on with his life. However Keith had slipped right out of the mainstream, not only in his academic attainments at school, but also in his social life.

He was now eighteen years old. His abilities enabled him to scrape the minimum pass levels in examinations. But Keith had lost interest in everything. Everything except drugs and Clare.

When Keith discovered that he could maintain a high, have less of a hangover and get even more into fantasy world with drugs, he thought he had found the answer to his problems. Now he had something to live for. Then Clare came along and for some reason unknown to him, she liked him. This was a miracle to Keith. Clare was by now one of the most important things in his life but she constantly found herself in competition with drugs. For Keith this caused major conflict. At times he felt he couldn't live without Clare, but at the same time he wanted to run from the hassle, the pressure she put on him. He knew he hurt her but he didn't want to stop using drugs. Keith was beginning to feel out of control.

These young people are a representative group of adolescents. They are facing major changes and choices in their life. In various ways they are at a crossroads and confused about the options facing them. They are not 'in between' lives, though

15

they are in between children and adults. They are very much alive with strong ideas, beliefs and feelings about the issues we all face. They are struggling to learn how to cope with life; with their bodies; with their urges and impulses, their emotions; with relationships, with new desires, new situations and new expectations and demands. They are also learning how to cope with mood-altering chemicals. The process of learning always involves making mistakes. The hope is that we learn from our mistakes, change our behaviour or thinking, and move on with more knowledge. This is the process that makes adolescence so painful. There is so much to be learned and there are so many different ways young people can make mistakes. So it is with their relationship with mood-altering chemicals: the possibilities for mistakes are limitless. Often young people themselves are unaware of the pitfalls ahead of them, happily ignorant or in denial of the dangers of the wrong choices.

Their parents, teachers or other concerned adults around them can usually see the possible mistakes only too clearly. Perhaps they have already learned from their own mistakes or have seen the consequences suffered by others. The dilemma for adults is how to negotiate this minefield, to steer and guide young people without removing their freedom to choose to learn. The temptation is to cocoon and protect but this could eventually stifle their growth and development in other areas. How can we help young people to recognise and respect the power and the danger of mood-altering chemicals and encourage and support them to say no? How can we help them to realise that drugs do not deliver the many things they seem to promise? How do we help them to recognise that rather than offering freedom and independence, drugs and alcohol lead to misery, captivity and dependence, to a more restricted life, rather than a better, wider one? How can we do this without pushing young people into corners where they feel they have no choices, no control over their life and that the only free choice left is rebellion by taking drugs and alcohol. If they are not given the freedom to say no for themselves, they may react by saying yes at a later stage, the only free choice they may perceive themselves as having.

At the other extreme is the danger of ignoring the warning signs and reacting too slowly to the indications that a young person has made mistakes and may not know how to extricate him- or herself from the dangerous situation.

The young people we have met are struggling to feel good about themselves. They are individuals who bring their personality, their family situation, their personal life history with them into their attempts to learn and develop. They are not at all the same and they do not all react in a similar way to the situations they find themselves in.

There are differences in their physical maturity and in their emotional maturity. Each of them approaches alcohol and drugs from an individual standpoint. They bring their own attitudes, thoughts and feelings and also their own personal beliefs, emotional needs and level of knowledge to bear on their decision. Their interaction with alcohol or drugs is basically a conflict situation for them. They each have a variety of different motivations concerning mood-altering chemicals. Some of these motivations may be in direct conflict with one another.

For example, Alice is sixteen years old. Her parents were concerned about her and did not want her to smoke cigarettes. They asked her not to. Alice loved her parents but wanted desperately to fit in with the other girls her own age. Nearly all the girls in her year had smoked since they were thirteen. Alice resisted for a period but then began to smoke cigarettes every now and then, particularly when out with her friends. She hid this from her parents and, once she reached sixteen, she began to recognise that she didn't need to smoke to belong with her friends. This freedom allowed her to question the faulty thinking which allowed her to worry about pollutants in the air, in her food and yet deny the danger of tobacco to her health and the fact that tobacco is also a drug. Alice was moving towards social maturity within her peer group and this relieved her of some of the pressures to smoke. But she found it harder than she expected to give it up.

As we have seen there is a wide range of motives behind teenagers using alcohol and drugs. Some of the reasons most commonly expressed by teenagers themselves are:

- To get a buzz
- To fit in
- To feel and look more mature

17

- To feel and look more attractive
- To keep up with their peers/friends and not seem too childish
- To have a sense of belonging to a group
- To smooth and make easier socialisation particularly with the opposite sex
- To be a man's man
- To build up their self-esteem
- To feel better about themselves
- To impress
- To block out feelings of inadequacy, loneliness, fear, anxiety
- To get spaced out
- Because everyone else is doing them
- Because there is nothing else to do
- For excitement and a sense of danger
- To rebel against parents and other adults

Of course these young people are in great danger because they are dealing with powerful psychoactive drugs, and that includes alcohol. Many teenagers listen to the information they are given and believe it. They react cautiously and question what is going on around them. They may be lucky enough to meet up with others who are not using drugs, who say, 'I don't need drugs'. But if they meet others who say, 'Try it. Everybody does it,' they may make up excuses to convince themselves why it is OK just to try it. They need to know that everybody doesn't do it, that alcohol and drugs are dangerous for their health. Sometimes they don't want to believe this because they want the immediate gratification rather than think of the long-term. They want the good feeling now, rather than remember the danger to their brain or their lungs.

They think: 'I've lots of time yet before they could do me any harm' or, 'Peter seems okay and he has used hash and acid.' Or, 'They're exaggerating; it has done Dick or Harry no harm.' Sometimes young people are in denial or even ignorance that they are more at risk than adults, that their bodies and minds are more vulnerable and that they can get addicted much faster than adults. Often they think 'I'm too young to become an alcoholic.'

Young people think that they won't ever lose control, that

they can take it or leave it. They don't realise, or they deny, the reality that eight out of ten young people who try even half a packet of cigarettes end up hooked for years or even their whole life. They may end up with cancer of the lungs or heart disease, and yet they tell themselves, 'Lots of people smoke, so what?'

Or when it comes to hash, pot or blow they say, 'It's not bad for you, it's only hash,' and try to believe it even though they may see friends losing interest in their school work and walking around half-dazed or slurring their words. Even though a component of hash can stay in the body for weeks even from one joint, dulling the ability to think clearly, remember or listen, they may convince themselves, 'It's only hash'. As someone once said, 'Whoever said smoking hash isn't bad for you must have smoked a little too much of it.' Often young people don't recognise alcohol as a drug either because it is so widely accepted socially.

'It is the *in* thing to do acid or Ecstasy,' is another favourite line from young people who are trying to convince themselves or others that it's OK. 'Try some speed or cocaine; you can always kick the habit.' What they often leave out or don't know is that these chemicals are addictive because after the buzz or high comes the crash or the low. After using them you feel worse and the more you use the worse you feel, the more drugs you need to lift you up out of the sickness, bad feelings and depression. Eventually anyone using drugs constantly doesn't enjoy them anymore. Young people need to know what they are in for if they use drugs, rather than just knowing that drugs are in.

Sometimes young people think they'll look bad if they say no. They don't realise that because it takes courage to stand up for what you believe in, they'll actually look good. They need to learn how to be assertive. To come up with another suggestion or change the subject or make a joke or look shocked when alcohol or drugs are even offered. Often they'll excuse their use of drugs by saying, 'I'm only trying it.' But you don't try getting hit by a lorry to find it's no fun and can hurt you. Young people need to be taught to talk out things that bother them, to develop relationships based on trust so that they don't need to turn to drugs for comfort, reassurance, confidence or to block out painful issues.

Chapter Three

Change

> 'How would you like to live in Looking-glass House,
> Kitty?... You can just see a little *peep* of the passage
> ...and it's very like our passage as far as you can see,
> only you know it may be quite different beyond... I'm
> sure it's got oh! such beautiful things in it ! Let's
> pretend there's a way of getting into it...Let's pretend
> the glass has got all soft so that we can get through...
>
> In another moment Alice was through the glass, 'I
> shall be as warm here as I was...warmer in fact because
> there'll be no-one here to scold me...Oh! what fun it'll
> be...'
>
> Lewis Carroll, *Through the Looking-Glass*

Often parents and family of a young person struggle to cope
with changes in physical appearance, mood swings,
personality shifts and often seemingly unpredictable
behaviour and attitudes, without recognising that much of this
is encompassed within the normal and necessary attempts to
manage the transition from a dependent, protected and
limited way of life to the independent, self-directed and
responsible lifestyle of a mature adult. The early, middle and
late stages of adolescence carry with them their own tasks as
does young adulthood. Often the accomplishment of
appropriate tasks lead to difficulties for young people and
their families because change is often difficult and usually
frightening or painful. Hormonal change in young people
often means that they are less easy-going and may be more
aggressive; parents and family usually find this new
moodiness and surliness difficult to live with. The need to be
an individual, not just one of the family, means that a young
person will experiment with dress, manners and habits of
behaviour in order to find a separate identity; parents
sometimes feel rejected and may have difficulty in giving their
child the space to be different from them.

If children are to become truly adult, not just physically

mature, they must within a few years achieve independence from their family, adjust to their sexual and physical maturation, form workable, meaningful and cooperative relationships with their peers, decide on and prepare for an adult occupation and develop a philosophy of life, that is a set of values and standards which will guide their behaviour. Most importantly, young people must develop a sense of identity, a sense of who they are, before they can safely abandon childhood. They must explore and discover where they are going and what their possibilities are. Exploration and discovery. Key words for all young people. Meanwhile we must never forget that every young person is first and foremost an individual, who will have to make their own personal journey to adulthood. Expectations based on parents' own needs or abilities may contribute to problems rather than help towards contentment. Young people need to be valued for what they are, recognised as being where they are on their own path without reference to others or comparisons with brothers, sisters, neighbours or friends.

Physical Change

'Curiouser and curiouser!' cried Alice...'Now I'm opening out like the largest telescope that ever was! Goodbye feet!'

Lewis Carroll, *Alice in Wonderland*

The physical change from child to adult is usually recognised to span the years from the onset of puberty to approximately the age of legal adulthood, from the age of ten to eighteen. For a few children the first signs of puberty (pubestas means 'age of manhood') can occur as early as the age of nine. Puberty is usually dated from the beginning of elevation of the breasts or onset of menstruation in girls, and the emergence of pigmented pubic hair in boys. First there is a growth spurt, with girls beginning two years earlier than boys, so that for a while they are both taller and heavier than their male coevals. The increase in height and weight varies widely from one child to another. The variation is unpredictable and can be different even within members of the same family. Very often, poor understanding of this fact causes needless distress both for young people and for their parents.

Puberty in girls usually begins at ten or eleven, with most

girls showing signs of development by thirteen and reaching full sexual maturity by the time they are sixteen. The sexual development of boys also begins later than girls', with most showing signs of development by the time they are fourteen and sexual maturity being reached at seventeen or eighteen. Again, all girls and boys should be made aware that the age of sexual maturation varies widely among normal young people; otherwise they may spend time worrying about their development.

The average young person is acutely and painfully aware of the entire growth process. The development of a sense of self, of recognition of one's own identity as a person requires a perception of oneself as

- Separate from others
- Being a whole person
- Having consistency over time

Commonsense will tell us that the many rapid changes in height, weight, body shape and dimensions that occur over such a short period of time can easily threaten a young person's sense of self-consistency. At the peak of his growth spurt, a boy may gain five to six inches in twelve months. At the same time there is an increased output of activating hormones which stimulate growth of bone, muscle and sexual characteristics, leading to changes in mood not previously experienced. It is no wonder that most early adolescents, like Alice in Wonderland look at the mirror and say ' Will the real me please stand up.' The rapidity of growth often means that young people are clumsy and uncoordinated and inconsequence extremely self-conscious. It is also not surprising that weight-watching is an almost universal preoccupation with young girls. They feel fatter because they *are* fatter, with muscle and fat being deposited in the breasts, hips and shoulders to give a rounded 'female' shape.

In the midst of so much change, it is crucial for young people to conform with something or be the same as someone. Because of this the movement towards their peer group, their coevals, as a source of security, status and conformity is increasingly important. They are less and less like children but not yet adult, and at least they are suffering the same changes as their peers, at least this is a group of individuals facing the same changes, fears, worries and anxieties as they are. However because of the different rates and speed of change, young people will still frequently be different from their friends and this can be an agonising, humiliating experience for them.

SAM

Sam struggles constantly with the fact that he is maturing slowly. At fourteen he is still very small in his class, his growth spurt only beginning. He will never be very tall anyway, having inherited his mother's family's genes and looking very like his maternal grandfather. At the moment he looks particularly small as some of his school friends are more than head and shoulders above him. He has been bullied by older boys in his area who jeer him and call him a girl, a gay, and a mammy's boy. He has grave, and for him very real, worries about his masculinity. And so he compensates by trying to be the macho guy, the hard man and uses cigarettes and alcohol to make his peers take him more seriously. Every morning Sam looks in the mirror and hates his boyish looks, while he carefully monitors the growth (non-existent!) on his upper lip.

For Sam as for many other young people, his view of his physical self is influenced also by past experiences. These can lead young people to view themselves as attractive or unattractive, masculine or feminine regardless of the actual facts of his or her appearance or capabilities. Even lads of average size and strength can view themselves as smaller or weaker than they are. Girls are even more conscious of their appearance and may think themselves 'ugly' because of comments made in the past.

Negative attitudes towards menstruation can affect a young girl's view of herself as a woman. Menstruation is a symbol of sexual maturity and parents can influence a girl's whole future sexual and social role as a woman by showing an understanding, caring attitude. Providing adequate medical care if there are physical difficulties, an explanation of the naturalness of the occurrence and showing pride and pleasure in a daughter's greater maturity can make menstruation a happy event. For boys nocturnal emissions can cause unnecessary fears if they do not receive proper instruction.

Late maturers are particularly at risk and need reassurance that the delay in their development is within normal expectations. Evidence from research indicates that later maturers are rated by their peers as less attractive, more affected and tense, more attention-seeking, restless and bossy and less popular. As one might expect, later maturers show more feelings of inadequacy, feelings of rejection and are often more rebellious. They score higher in the feelings of guilt, inferiority, depression and anxiety and have a greater need for encouragement and sympathy.

For girls, early maturity can bring its problems also. They may become less popular with girlfriends who are still pubertal. It is only when their peers also begin to cope with the demands of puberty that the picture shifts and they can reap the benefit of early maturity.

JANE

Jane found herself at ten, eleven and twelve years of age treated with suspicion by her still childlike and, to her, childish friends. Her body looked adult and this created a divide between herself and her peers. She found herself feeling different and looking different. Jane became very self-conscious and developed a way of walking with her head down and shoulders hunched which made her look smaller and her breasts less conspicuous. She felt huge and was extremely clumsy, always knocking down things and banging into people. For Jane cigarettes and alcohol brought her into a peer group where she seemed to belong.

TOM

Of course a young person may be physically mature but not emotionally mature. Tom is a good example of this. Tom looked fifteen when he was twelve years old. However he had an emotional age of about 10 and often acted like a ten-year-old. He is an only child, and his parents were very proud of their fine, healthy, strapping young man. Tom looked so tall, so grown-up, and both Val and Sheila had great hopes and plans for him. Inside Tom was frightened. He was slow in school and struggled to keep up with his classmates. They thought him very silly, though often good for a laugh and a bit of distraction as he clowned his way through classes. Tom was out of his depth long before anyone realised it.

While growth is occurring, the so-called 'body-schema' which gives us a conception of the position of our body and our limbs, and on the basis of which we judge our position in relation to surrounding objects, is partially lost. It is characteristic at this stage to stumble and knock things over. It is difficult for a young person who is growing rapidly to remember where the different parts of their body are. Yes, he may not know that his feet are placed right on your foot or she may not realise that her elbow needs to be moved so that she can sit comfortable beside her sister at the dinner table.

Rapid physical growth involves many forms of strain. Restlessness and fatigue are partly due to physical causes. More calories are needed. Eating habits are often more irregular during these years than at any other time. The course of sexual maturation gives rise to strong forces of motivation which lead to new channels of behaviour. Sexual impulses and fantasies are strong. The level of education and availability of information have consequences for a young person's sexual and social role as a man or a woman. If young people do not receive instruction they may torture themselves with worry and a sense of helplessness may stem from this. Sexual education increases the individual's understanding of both the biological and social condition of human beings. Feelings of right and wrong which have a restraining influence and are conditioned by responsibility are not harmful but assets. Young people need to learn how to take responsibility for themselves, to act responsibly towards themselves and others. Man is a biological creature but has also the privilege of becoming, with the help of his reason, a socially creative person.

Intellectual Change

'How queer everything is today ! And yesterday things went on just as usual. I wonder if I've been changed in the night? Let me think: *was* I the same when I got up this morning? I almost think I can remember feeling a little different. But if I'm not the same, the next question is 'Who in the world am I?' Ah *that's* the great puzzle!'
Lewis Carroll, *Alice's Adventures in Wonderland*

During these years young people's intellectual and cognitive abilities are changing also. The ways they think and what they think about are altered. This is a very important aspect of the changes in both personality and behaviour. They are now able to think abstractly, to ponder and to grasp not only the present, the 'here and now' but also the possible, or how things might be or could be. Without these formal operations (Piaget's 'second-degree' operations), the ability to think about statements that have no relation to real objects, they would not be able to master calculus, for example, or understand the use of metaphor in poetry. Neither would they be capable of meeting the increasingly complex demands being made on them to deal with the world.

Young people will inevitably make use of their newly discovered talents in challenging their parents' thoughts, attitudes and values and this may be very wearing. Often they will relentlessly criticise politicians, the church, school and other symbols of authority, renouncing them as hypocritical or corrupt. Their new awareness of the difference between the possible and the actual may make them rebels. They compare their parents constantly to others, often labelling them 'square' or more/less understanding. It is difficult but essential to remember that there are positive aspects to this: they are reasoning every which way, exploring, hypothesising about ideas, ideals and values in order to make the choices that pave the way into mature adulthood.

JOHN

Take John for example. He was a happy, placid child, easy to rear, and his parents never really reflected on their good fortune or good parenting but got on with the job. They are an easygoing couple with few disruptions to their way of life, happily married with only the usual disagreements and ups and downs. In lots of ways John mirrored their attitudes. To their horror, when he was about eleven, he became rebellious, defiant and rude, and convinced he was not getting a fair deal. He started getting into minor rows at school with endless stories about how unfairly he had been treated by his teacher when he had only been doing the same as everyone else. John seemed to see everyone as against him if they didn't immediately take his side and agree totally with him. This was a dramatic change from the compliant child.

Of course John was simply beginning to deal with hormonal and physical changes and asserting himself as a person with his own views. This was so new for him he was going overboard and was unable to compromise. 'Intolerant' was the best word for his opinions, and his parents were often shocked by his views of other people: his friends, his brothers and sisters and even them. Indeed he seemed to compare them constantly to his friends' parents rather than thinking them the best in the world as he had always done. John's parents were hurt by all this and felt criticised and rejected but also irritated by his constant demands for more freedom, more money. They felt used and found it difficult to detach him from his bad temper and moodiness.

This continued for three to four years with occasional lulls. In the last year—John is now sixteen—they have noticed that he definitely seems more reasonable and tolerant and will now at least listen to others' opinions. However this does not mean he is any more biddable. If anything, John is more reluctant to let his parents interfere in his life or make decisions for him. His friends are increasingly important to him and he is determined to do what he wants in terms of clothes, hairstyles, entertainment. His parents are now learning to let go and are working on trusting him. This is very frightening for them, especially since some of his opinions and choices of fashion seem way-out, bizarre. They need to realise this is an experimental stage and that very likely none of these 'roles' is permanent. His questioning of their standards and values is particularly worrying for them because John is rejecting their religious views. He is also spending less and less time with them and more and more 'out' with his friends. Like many other mothers with children of this age, June complains that John treats the house 'like a hotel'. He will not even talk to her about his girlfriend and she worries about how secretive he is. She worries that he will get his girlfriend pregnant. June also worries that John is drinking and that he might drink too much.

John is experimenting with a self-image, testing his boundaries and taking risks. He is starting to make more intimate friendships and also accepting his sexuality by forming relationships which involve new, private feelings he has never had before. He is also learning to think independently and to make his own decisions. The changes occurring in John are not only natural but essential for his growth, but this does not mean they are not difficult, even painful for the rest of the family.

It is important for John to recognise that it is a time of change for his parents also and that they need time to adjust also. He needs to remember that though they may make mistakes, they are basically on his side. He should not assume that if he has a problem they wouldn't understand or be prepared to help him. It is a hard time for them: his father is finally facing up to the fact that he has gone as far as he will ever go on the promotion ladder and his mother's role is becoming redundant as his younger siblings get bigger. It is a time of change in their life also. John's father in particular is struggling as he sees his eldest son reach manhood with all the possibilities of life before him, all the opportunities for sexual partners, all the potential paths John could take for a career still open. Jack sees his own possibilities narrowing and there are strains of envy within the hope and desire for a good life for his son. He cannot understand John's fascination with the stage and theatre and fears that he will mess up his academic standing and miss secure, financially viable vocations. Jack, of course, needs support to recognise that John may have inclinations, abilities and talents beyond his understanding or interest. The hardest task of all for Jack and June is to stand by and watch John become more physically and socially daring, taking risks by acting independently and doing things which they know only too well are dangerous. Even mature young people think they are immortal and too young to die, to get AIDS, to become addicted. Young people will often disregard safety precautions and warnings in the search for adventure, excitement and pleasure. June and Jack want to discourage and advise John but they know this may antagonise him.

Young people often appear egocentric and self-centred. They are increasingly introspective and analytical, often preoccupied with thought itself. Long stretches of time are spent just 'thinking', staring into space, listening to music, writing poetry or just lying in their bed for hours on end. Why am I like this? they think and Who is it who is thinking, why am I like this? and who is it who is thinking, who is it who is thinking why am I like that?

Because of the painful self-awareness that stems from the rapid physical and psychological changes such as this increasing intellectual awareness, the focus of young people's concern tends to be upon themselves. Since they often cannot differentiate between their concerns and the concerns of others, they are likely to conclude that other people are just as obsessed with their behaviour and appearance as they are. As in very early childhood, an adolescent is once again centre-stage and he or she spends most of time preparing his entrance, his costume and his reactions for his audience.

Of course although he or she feels all eyes are on him, this is rarely the case, and when a group of young people meet they are more likely to be preoccupied with themselves than observing others. The most fun part of such a gathering for a young person can often be the trying on of different outfits, the changing of hairstyles from one way to another, the endless hours in the bathroom or bedroom in front of the mirror, preparing for the dramatic impression they will make. When they are feeling down or self-critical, they will also believe their audience will be critical also. This leads to greater anxiety and self-consciousness. The use of alcohol and drugs is obviously attractive to young people for these reasons because by using them they can become less sensitive to others' reactions and experience a bubble of drug-induced good feelings. Mood-altering chemicals provide a welcome relief from their primary concern, that is, what or how they appear to others, rather than what they feel they are.

Young people are lovers of irony and of the 'put down' and delight in double entendres, in jokes, hidden agendas and the humour of the absurd. Again, these are opportunities to demonstrate and practise new skills, but they can be tiresome and annoying to live with. However, the fun and delight shared with young people when they are enjoying themselves can be exhilarating. There is an energy and excitement pouring from their pleasure in their new talents and abilities to think in new ways.

Their emerging awareness of how things might be in contrast to how they are can lead to very real dissatisfaction and even depression for young people. For those for whom life has presented deficits, problems and disadvantages, awareness brings more hurt, sorrow and anger. Not surprisingly the oblivion of mood-altering chemicals, tempting for all people struggling with the normal pressures and difficulties of life, can be irresistibly seductive for young people facing their first taste of real depression.

Young people need warm, loving, supportive relationships in their lives in order that they may have these tools which will equip them to deal with the obstacles on the road to healthy, contented maturity. Dependency on mood-altering chemicals such as alcohol or other drugs can halt a young person's development. Unfortunately a relationship with drugs may itself be an attempt to cope with the tasks and trials of the path through adolescence.

Chapter Four

Conflicts and Resolutions

Independence

Much of the behaviour of young people as they move from childhood to adulthood seems incomprehensible and baffling for adults. Adults may see no redeeming feature in the choices their adolescents or young adults are making. Often this is because they don't understand the reasons for them and may believe there are no reasons.

Take rebelliousness for example. Parents often say that they are frustrated and angered by the way young people act in a rebellious manner. But rebellion is the first sign of children's drive for independence. They need to be different from their parents and to establish their own identity. Initially they may go overboard, and even choose to do things not because they really want to but because they know their parents don't want them to. If young people simply comply and don't act in a way that shows determination to be separate from their parents they may be missing a necessary stage in their development towards mature adulthood. Within their rebellion young people are still desirous of their parents' love and support. Finding out who they are, separate from their parents, also means believing that they are lovable, worthwhile and important as themselves and not just as offspring or offshoots of their parents.

The development of independence is central to the task of becoming adult. Developing a reasonable separation from their parents and a sense of autonomy influences many areas:

- Self-reliance
- Profitable peer relationships
- Mature sexual relationships
- Confident pursuit of a vocation
- Adequate financial independence and a positive sense of identity

Negotiating progress towards these goals involves conflict for young people in countries like ours, where they are expected to move from relatively great dependence on their family to considerable independence within a demanding and complex society. Often no clear pattern of transition from dependence to independence is spelt out, with expectations of individuals at various ages varying from parent to parent, family to family and situation to situation.

Chris, Keith and Anna are part of the same peer group, living in the same area and attending the same school. They are all approximately the same age, eighteen, with Anna a few months younger. They are young adults at this point in their lives.

CHRIS

Chris's family has a myriad problems. His father is alcoholic and he has two elder brothers still living at home, one unemployed. In many ways Chris is treated like an adult. Rarely is he questioned about what he is doing or where he is going. On the surface of things he seems independent, self-reliant and with no cribs to his choices. He is articulate and charming and appears sure of himself. However because of the lack of boundaries and expectations, and lacking structured evidence of parental care and concern, Chris is finding it difficult to define himself in relation to his parents, to measure his progression towards independence and to set goals of financial, emotional and vocational independence. Because no one seems to care about him or to limit him, Chris has no sense of being important, and little awareness of his achievements. For most young people, boundaries and limits make possible a sense of growth and development, a way of measuring their movement towards maturity. Though they strain at the leash and champ on the bit, they mostly recognise that these are signs that their parents care, and despite rows, rebellions and arguments, most young people would describe their relationship with their parents as one of concern and love.

Chris's mother is distressed and unwell. Her health has crumbled due to her preoccupation with her husband's drinking and behaviour and she is too tired, too busy or too worried to pay attention to Chris's pursuits. She plays a passive role in the home, spending her days cleaning, cooking, shopping and trying to keep the four men in her life happy. Chris has received little encouragement to become financially independent. His mother gives him whatever she can when he asks, and he regularly steals money from his dad when his dad is drunk. Chris believes he is entitled to it because his dad would only drink it and anyway his dad rarely, if ever, notices that he is short a few quid. Because of the turmoil caused by his dad and one of his elder brothers who also pursues a life centred on the pub, Chris's behaviour usually escapes unnoticed. Nothing is expected from him at home either in terms of pulling his weight in the house, doing chores or behaving responsibly towards his family. On the other hand he is seen as entitled to drive the family car (when he is lucky enough to get it), stay out as late as he wants at night and pretty much live his own life.

Chris's drinking started as an attempt to become adult, to join his dad and brother on their own ground. As he was already struggling in school, the comfort of moving into a peer group where brownie points came from handling your drink rather than from how you performed in class was irresistible. He was also attracted to the company of older lads. To be accepted by them was again a comfort when he was constantly rejected, dismissed and even ignored at home as being only 'the young one'. Chris moved quickly into drugs and then harder drugs.

He has used dependence on mood-altering chemicals as a way of coping with his dependency needs for acceptance and approval, to measure and signal his coming of age.

KEITH

At the same age, Keith is expected to play an active role in financing himself. He has had a part-time job since he was thirteen, starting with a paper delivery, then a job in the local garage shop. He now works in the supermarket three nights a week and all day Saturday. Because his father is not around, Keith's mother depends on him to help around the house, make meals, do the garden, mind the younger children. She watches Keith constantly, questioning him about friends, particularly girls, about what he is doing, where he is going and when he is coming back. Keith was always quiet and shy and his mother's constant concern about his affairs has made his attempts at socialising even more difficult. He, in turn worries about his mother and knows that she will be watching the clock, waiting for him. He never feels free to be his own person. Now that he is going out with Clare he feels even more under pressure. Firstly he is trying to keep the relationship private, away from his mother's interference. Secondly he wants more and more to spend time with Clare and this leads to conflict with his commitments at home.

Keith, like Chris, is using alcohol and drugs, in an unhealthy way. For Keith, alcohol and drugs have become a haven from his conflicting and ambivalent feelings towards his family. He loves his family but feels trapped by them. He too has dependency needs which have not been met as he was catapulted into adulthood and responsibility while craving security and safety, becoming his mother's confidante and companion while he still needed to be free from responsibility. His attempts to rebel and pull against his mother in order to become a separate individual have been thwarted both by his own guilt and concern over the family and her needs and dependence on him. Keith has moved into drinking to the point of oblivion and taking drugs in order to escape from his overwhelming feelings of fear, anxiety, anger and hopelessness. He has also become dependent on Clare and clings to her possessively, which is already causing major difficulties between them.

ANNA

Anna faces her own problems. She comes from a happy and comfortable home and had a childhood that could only be described as idyllic but because she is an only child, her parents have focused much of their life, goals, aspirations and dreams on her. They smother her in love and provide for her every need. As is the case for Chris, pocket money is no problem.

Her mother and father love to see her dressed prettily and enjoying herself. They take a great interest in her friends, hobbies and school work. They encourage her in her special talent for music and are very clear about limits in terms of where she can go, who she can be with and what time she gets in. Anna loves her parents dearly and delights in pleasing them but she is feeling increasingly trapped. This year her parents have yet again planned an exotic Continental holiday but Anna does not want to go with them. She would much prefer to go youth-hostelling in the country with her two friends and maybe even her new boyfriend, Chris. She does not want her parents to know everything about her; she needs to have some secrets, something that is just hers. She is reluctant to show her feelings because she does not want to hurt them. In other ways she believes she owes them; after all they give her everything.

Anna has never been encouraged to become financially independent. She has no savings or earnings of her own and she often feels controlled by her parents. She knows they would give her anything she asks for but she hates having to ask. She wishes she either earned a set amount from them by doing chores or had a job out of the house. At least then her money would be her own. But her parents will not allow her to get a job because they want her to practise the piano, and believe she cannot do both. Anna does not want to be treated as if she has no ideas, thoughts or plans of her own but arguments and rows seem to make her parents firmer in their decisions about what she can and can't do.

Increasingly Anna is choosing to wear scruffy and casual clothes which shock her father in particular. He seems to want her to be his 'pretty girl' and Anna is getting angrier and angrier about it. The more she tries to assert herself as a separate person the more her parents use her sense of guilt 'to get their way'. Anna has resorted to dishonesty and mood-altering chemicals in attempt to find freedom and independence. She believes her parents are interfering, treating her like a child, and wishes they would leave her alone. The risk, excitement and apparent freedom of alcohol and drugs seem very alluring to her, as does the danger involved in dating Chris, the wild boy of the area.

Young people have problems not just in achieving independence because of inconsistencies around them but also because they themselves experience conflict. One part of them wants to be independent and the other part desires security and lack of responsibility. For this reason they are particularly at risk of becoming dependent on mood-altering chemicals such as alcohol, cannabis, amphetamines, heroin. Drugs offer a seemingly predictable and guaranteed escape.

They offer excitement, freedom, danger and comfort—all at a set price. Or so it appears at first.

The lure and false promise of psychoactive drugs is a trap for young people, just as it is for their elders. The damage is, if anything, greater, because dependency on alcohol and drugs stops emotional development in its tracks. There is many a forty-year old alcoholic who starts to recognise as he enters recovery that inside he is still the fourteen-year-old boy who drank to become a 'man'.

In most western societies there is no clear rite of passage that marks the entrance to manhood or womanhood. In other cultures, (sometimes called primitive) there are rituals and celebrations that define and mark the beginning of adulthood. In the west, the age at which a person can drive, marry, vote, drink alcohol legally all vary from country to country. Confusion is the norm, and families and young people are thrown on their own resources to find a way to negotiate this passage. Research has indicated that confidence and self-esteem are highest in young people whose parents express interest in and knowledge of their opinions and activities but also encourage independent self-directed behaviour and participation in family activities and decisions. Communication, opportunities for independence with appropriate degrees of control and parents who are positive models of flexible, problem-solving behaviour—these, as well as love and security, seem to provide the optimum background for development of responsible independence. But parents cannot provide detailed blueprints.

Neither is there any such thing as an ideal parent. At best, members of families can make each other feel valued. Parents can listen to their young son or daughter, work out decisions within set limits, but respond to reasonable demands. The chances are that because different children respond differently, parents can never be equally successful with all their children. All they can do is try and treat them consistently, fairly and as individuals.

Peers

Young people's social development is mostly worked out within their peer group. If they are to feel at home in the adult world it is of fundamental importance that they are initiated into and accepted by their peers. Belonging to a group is usually regarded by young people as being of the greatest significance. Throughout adolescence and into young adulthood, young people become less family-centred and more friend-centred. Their friends play a larger role in their life and their relations with members of the same or opposite sex form prototypes for adult relationships in social settings, in work and in sexual relationships. Girls tend to form a few special friendships without which life seems to be unbearable. They spend hours on the phone, endlessly chatting to their 'best friends'. For lads, having a special friend may not be as important as being accepted by a particular group or gang.

Often young people reject the family because to act independently of it may increase prestige among companions of their own age. Young people try to the best of their ability to play the part demanded by their peers. Ties with parents become progressively looser as they attempt to bond more closely with others of their own age. Their sense of identity is so fluid that 'being the same as' within the group helps them to define it. Young people need, more than at any time in their life, to be able to share their strong and often confusing emotions, their doubts and their dreams. Relationships with the family tend to be painful because of conflicting feelings and many aspects of their inner life become difficult to share with their family. Often parents are not able to cope with the intense, painful feelings of this time. So for young people, their peer group is a place where others are experiencing at least the same struggle. Adults have already 'arrived', and no matter how understanding parents may be, this limits their role. Adolescence is a time of intense loneliness. Merely being with a crowd does not solve the problem, but being accepted by the crowd, and having one or a couple of close friends, can make all the difference.

JOHN

John's parents are horrified at his clothes, hairstyle and choice of music. To them, he looks like a clown or a tramp with dark, shapeless clothes and messy hair. His music is just noise. They have known for a few years that his shoes, his trousers or his jacket have just to be the 'right' kind or he will not wear them. The 'right' kind can change practically overnight, and what he was begging for one week, he will pronounce old or sick the next week. June grumbles constantly to Jack: 'They all look the same; I can't see the difference between his old black top and his new one. Why won't he wear it?' This stage will not last for ever, and eventually John will have the desire to look like an individual. But for now it is still important for him to have the 'cloak of invisibility' around him—to look like everyone else, at least everyone who matters to him. These things are not little things to John. It matters a lot to him that he looks, sounds and acts just right. In matter of values and understanding of the adult world, John actually gravitates towards Jack and June. They are a solid rock for him. The influence of his friends tends to be limited to such matters as taste in music and style.

For other, less lucky young people who have a more shaky family background, suffering from parental disregard or lack of attention (for example Chris), the vacuum caused by the absence of parents is often filled by peers and may result in more fundamentally antisocial behaviour such as 'doing something illegal' or 'mitching school'. The importance of peer approval varies from individual to individual. Some few may not need or seek the opinion of their peers. But most, still judging their own worth to a considerable extent in terms of others' reactions to them, are dependent on the approval and acclaim of prestigious peers. This becomes particularly difficult and sensitive where members of the opposite sex are concerned. Unfortunately if a young person is already emotionally troubled, preoccupied with himself and lacking in a secure self-concept he is likely to meet with rejection or indifference from his peers. Awareness of this lack of opportunities to participate in and learn from wholesome healthy peer group activities further undermines his self-confidence and increases his sense of social isolation. This may result in further inappropriate behaviour with his peers.

SAM

Sam feels very self-conscious, is full of insecurities and doubts. He is unpopular at school. He resorts to clowning and making inane comments and jokes in order to become liked. He spends a lot of time chatting up the girls. The lads in his year think him stupid and silly and the girls dismiss him and say that his house smells. They know he is a bit different—after all he is adopted—but they would not think or say this is why he is not liked. Sam and his peers are caught in an all too common vicious circle. He is needy, insecure and tries too hard. His companions pick these vibes up and are uncomfortable with his lack of confidence. To make matters worse he lives away from the area and falls between two stools when it comes to social occasions. He cannot go to activities in the area where he goes to school, and he is more an outsider, and knows even fewer people, where he lives. Sam is very much at risk. He is isolated and has already discovered alcohol as a companion.

Few young people are unaffected by social neglect, rejection or censure. To be part of a minority group or from a socially disapproved-of background causes inner pain and difficulties. Some will try to cope with their discomfort by being overly conceited or demanding of attention. Another behaviour which may be an attempt to compensate for perceived social deficits is aggressiveness. Sometimes young people act in a tactless, inconsiderate, even abusive manner, verbally or physically. This will increase the chances of their being rejected by their peers and lead to further alienation.

When young people are behaving rudely or aggressively it can be caused by thoughtlessness or shyness, unhappiness or anxiety. If they feel frustrated, think that they are not being listened to or are being treated unfairly, they may also act in a verbally aggressive manner. It is important for adults to be sensitive to these matters and to be aware that young people may be finding it hard to say how they are feeling. Kindness, sympathy or just listening may help. Unfortunately, aggression can become a habitual response if issues are not recognised or resolved.

PATRICK

Patrick, at seventeen, is the local drug dealer. This means that he always has a supply of hash, acid and speed at hand. He is the go-between for the local kids and a more deeply involved dealer. He can fill out special orders for anyone with only a days' notice. Patrick became enmeshed with the heavies to feed his own habit. He is an unknown quantity for most people. Surly, rude and very withdrawn, Patrick does not socialise. He keeps to his chosen inner circle and interacts with others on a 'need-to' basis. He is quick to threaten and his manner is aggressive not only because of his tone but also his use of obscenities and the content of his conversation. He carries a knife and lets everyone know that he would like to use it. At heart Patrick is a very confused and unhappy individual. His parents are totally distracted by his behaviour but quite frightened of by him, just like other people. Patrick is dependent on drugs and his personality is now very distorted, even dangerous.

Sexuality

An acknowledgement by young people of their sexuality and the development of ability to act in a more confident, comfortable, responsive and intimate way with members of the opposite sex are concomitants of the task of sexual maturation that is addressed during the years of adolescence. For girls, heterosexual attraction comes earlier than for boys, but the rapid increase in sexual drive for boys is practically impossible to deny. For lads the sexual drive is biologically specific and needs to be discharged without excessive guilt. For girls the romantic relationship usually takes precedence, with the fulfilment of needs such as self-esteem, reassurance, affection coming first. The overall relationship is more important, something that helps girls control their sexual impulses. Masturbation is very common. Research indicates that about 60% of girls masturbate. How young people cope with this aspect of their lives depends on family expectations and restrictions as well as society's influences. Initially younger adolescents may be embarrassed and worry about sexual matters, for example the size and shape of their sexual organs. How much young people experiment depends on:

- What society expects
- Their morals and religious beliefs
- Their emotional readiness

If a relationship moves into physical intimacy too soon, pressures and guilt may result. The need for intimacy, to be close to someone special, to belong with someone else rather than feel alone, curiosity, the desire to take control of their lives and bodies, to taste forbidden fruit and to be the same as

40

others—all these are factors that move a young person towards sexual activity.

For all of us, sexuality is a vulnerable, personal and difficult issue. Our sense of self is fundamentally linked with in our sexual self. One of the earliest labels or definitions we learn to place on ourselves is our sex or gender. In this area, as in other areas, young people want to be independent, 'normal', or the same as everyone else, and confident. However, it can often be difficult to work out what 'healthy' sexuality means. This is because sex is an intensely private matter. It is important, therefore, for parents to accept their children's developing sexuality and to make sure they are well informed. Young individuals should know more than just the basic mechanics of sex and should be educated about how men and women respond emotionally to each other as well as physically. Contraception and the risks of sexually transmitted disease are important issues. These are difficult and awkward topics but young people may be too frightened or anxious to ask, especially when they do face a problem.

Young people need also to be made aware of the implications of emotional readiness for a sexual relationship, respect and responsibility towards each other, and the role of permanent relationships within the context of religious and moral belief systems. If young people are sensible and responsible in other areas, they tend to be sensible and responsible in their sexual lives too. Friendships with members of the opposite sex are usually the beginnings of sexual relationships. Though these may not last long, they are important. Young people need to move in and out of relationships but some become involved in very intense relationships very early. These are usually young people who are having difficulties in dealing with their dependency needs and in detaching from their parents. Feelings are very strong and they suffer real misery when even seemingly casual relationships break up. Pretending that nothing is happening does not help young people; neither does a 'tell-me-everything' approach. The most sound and realistic approach is for parents to express honestly their fears for the young person, for example pregnancy, the distraction from other opportunities, the dangers of too-early marriage and the addictive qualities of sexual experiences. Young people may

41

then recognise the wisdom of postponing sex for a while.

The use of alcohol and drugs often compromises a young person's developing sexuality. Often the removal of rational judgement and the anaesthetising of feelings which usually results from using powerful mood-altering chemicals mean that young people can end up either abusing their own sexuality or putting themselves in situations where they are at risk of being abused. The evidence indicates that young people who move into a regular relationship with alcohol usually become sexually active earlier than others.

ANNA

Anna has been seriously confused, unhappy and ashamed since her last experiment with alcohol and drugs. She had a blackout on that particular occasion, which means that though she acted and behaved as if everything was OK, and though she was fully conscious, her brain did not record what occurred. An amnesiac episode like this is very common when someone has become chemically dependent but can also occur when someone uses an unusually high amount of alcohol or combines it with other drugs. Anna had used alcohol, hash [cannabis] and also taken some unknown tablets. What happened that night? She knew Chris had been out of his head also and that he had a very confused, even unreal notion of the night's events. Tessa had been very solicitous and Anna had done her best to keep her at a distance. Meanwhile her sense of panic and anxiety was escalating. Where did they go? What had she done? Who was she with? Finally Tessa managed to catch Anna in a corner and yet again she said, 'Are you all right?'

'Of course I'm all right,' Anna replied, but worry got the upper hand and she asked, 'What do you mean?'

'Don't you know what I mean? What about the night of the exam results? Are you all right?'

'What do you mean?' Anna again asked and Tessa sighed. 'You don't remember do you? Do you?' When Anna shook her head Tessa took a deep breath. 'You went off with two of the guys that night. At different times! You were staggering and totally spaced out but you kept saying "It's OK, it's cool," so I left you alone.' Again Anna heard herself say, 'What do you mean I was with two guys?'

'Well, we were at Peter's house and you went upstairs with that tall guy. The one who always wears the patched denim jacket—you know the one with the blonde hair. Later you went upstairs with Jake, Patrick's mate. Chris was passed out in the kitchen from early on.' Anna whispered, 'What do you mean, I went upstairs?'

'Well, I don't know,' Tessa replied, 'I just know I saw you go upstairs with them! Are you all right? By this stage Anna was white as a sheet. She didn't know herself if she was all right but she knew only too well what Tessa was asking. Her periods were always a bit irregular but…'Will you come to the chemist in town with me, Tessa?'

'It's a bit late now, don't you think?'

'Well I think I'll get a predictor kit…just in case.'

As she rode into town on the bus to buy her pregnancy-testing kit, Anna swore that she would never, ever, ever, drink again. She prayed long and hard that she would get a second chance, that she wouldn't be pregnant, that her parents wouldn't have to know, that she would be able to do her exams, that she could try to be a concert pianist. She also felt sick and disgusted with herself. She couldn't have done *that*, could she? Surely she would have known. She wanted her first time to be special, not dirty, underhand and drunken. That would make her a slut wouldn't it, to be drunk, not to remember, and to be with two guys?

Whatever happened for Anna as a long-term result of that evening the consequences of alcohol and drugs were at very least, guilt, shame, worry, anxiety and a lowered self-esteem. For other young people, experimentation with or dependency on alcohol and drugs affects their sexual maturation and development because it encourages ill-considered and uninhibited acting out of strong and powerful impulses and drives while under the influence of drink or drugs, early sexual experimentation while emotionally immature, abusing sexuality for highs or to get money for alcohol and drugs.

As young people move toward young adulthood a related task is to settle down, develop more meaningful and committed interpersonal relationships and move towards marriage and parenthood. The restlessness, searching and experimentation of adolescence need to be relinquished for responsibility and commitment. If young people are investing an inordinately large portion of their time, energy, money and effort into their relationship with mood-altering chemicals they are most probably dependent on them, that is, addicted. This can sap their interest, connection and relationship with other people and leave them detached, self- centred and insensitive.

Vocation

A fourth critical developmental task of adolescence and young adulthood is settling on and working towards a vocation, career or job. The identification of young people with adult roles is inextricably connected with this task and the choice of a vocation and participation in the workforce helps to shape and strengthen a young person's self-concept and self-image. Work gives us a sense of importance, of being needed, of being part of something, of having a purpose in life. This leads to major difficulties and concerns for our young people in a society where work is not freely available and where there is less and less work for unskilled or semi-skilled workers. There is more pressure within the educational system to train and specialise. for all sorts of reasons:

- Individual ability
- Family situation
- Socio-economic group or background

The use of alcohol and drugs can seriously undermine young people's abilities and talents and weaken their energy and interest in their education. Their attitude towards school authorities and parents who advocate placing greater priority on study can cause great conflict in situations where young people are becoming reliant on alcohol and drugs.

Keith is a bright, intelligent young man but his grades have fallen dramatically. He has lost his interest, his enthusiasm for anything other than drink, drugs and Clare. He gets by because he is clever but he is not achieving anything like his potential. Chris's interest in a job is minimal. He is not even planning to provide for his future but lives for his next joint, can of beer or rush from speed. Tom has completely lost sight of any educational goals though he still has a fantasy about working with his dad. In reality he too lives from drink to drink and is not even working towards getting the minimum exam results required to go for an apprenticeship. Tessa takes no interest in her schoolwork and dreams the days away, popping into the toilets every few hours to smoke hash. The relationship these young people have with alcohol and drugs is weakening their desire and ability to work on the development of vocational goals.

Identity
At the core of the various tasks in the years of transition towards adulthood is the development of a sense of identity, a clear image and definition of oneself as a person. They help young people to form a conception of themselves with some positive and some negative aspects. In choosing hairstyles, clothes and music as well as friends, sexual partners, interests and opinions, attitudes and values, young people are deciding who they are, or perhaps more accurately who they want to be. The use of alcohol and drugs at this critical crossroads in their life complicates and confuses their emotions and their thoughts about the choices facing them.

A good analogy for the movement towards adulthood is that of the expulsion of Adam and Eve from the Garden of Eden. Most children begin life in a sort of family Eden and then undergo the pain of separation from their parents as they assume more responsibility for their lives. From living in a safe environment with needs met and boundaries clearly drawn, Adam and Eve were given the opportunity to make choices. With that gift came the power of love, the chance to enjoy friendship but also to experience pain and grief, the necessity to work, to have children and responsibilities. So it is for the challenges young individuals face as they grow from simple obedience to freedom of choice. This is painful though exciting and rewarding. The development of independent social and moral choice involves influences within and outside the family. Adolescence and young adulthood is a difficult time in what often appears a lonely and threatening word. The proper goal for each individual is to gain relative independence but this also involves the loss of a 'paradisaical' state which was relatively free of conflict, guilt and self-awareness. It is exchanged for:

- Conflicting demands on time and loyalty
- The need to make important decisions with far-reaching

consequences for the whole of one's life
- Pressure to make these decisions quickly and sometimes with insufficient information
- Powerful physical changes and urges

A huge task, difficult for all. For some individuals the temptation to give up the task and seek oblivion and comfort in either alcohol or narcotics is overwhelming. Some young people are motivated by already existing hopelessness or seek a way out of the demands of developing maturity. For other young people simple curiosity or pleasure-seeking brings them down the road to the isolation, despair and emptiness of drug dependency.

Chapter Five

Types and categories of drugs

You meet someone and they say, 'Did you hear about Tony? He's on drugs.' Depending on who you are, what your experiences have been, what age you are or where you live, you will react with emotion ranging from lack of surprise, to lack of interest, to sadness, to shock and horror. The chances are, though, that you will immediately think of what are generally known as 'hard' drugs such as heroin or cocaine.

The reality is that our lives are full of substances that bring about changes in our emotions, our behaviour and our bodily functions. All these substances can be classified as drugs, though many people would not readily consider them as such. Indeed people often rely on drugs to get them through the day, to improve or change their feelings and to comfort and reward themselves. Tea and coffee are examples of beverages which are taken to act as pick-me-ups. Other cold drinks such as colas also contain caffeine, the mild stimulant that is contained in tea and coffee.

People will take drugs without thinking, buying them over the counter to deal with minor ailments. These remedies are purchased for pain relief, to treat colds, to help with anxiety and insomnia, for stomach aches and headaches. In general these over-the-counter drugs are effective and safe, but sometimes they can be abused without much awareness of what is happening. The ready availability and glossy marketing of such products reflects society's acceptance of and demand for 'a pill for every ill'.

Alcohol and tobacco are two other examples of everyday drugs which clearly affect mood, mind and body. Both relax the user, reduce tension and provide an initial and immediate stimulation. Both cause serious physical damage and are frequently abused. Both are psychologically addictive yet legal and relatively socially acceptable.

The term 'drugs' also conjures up the vast array of products that are invaluable for specific medicinal purposes including treating disease, reducing pain and counteracting nervous disorders and depression. Unfortunately these too can be used for non-medical purposes.

In order to understand the dynamics of how young people move into the misuse and abuse of psychoactive drugs it is important that we recognise that we are living within a drug culture, where some drugs are not only accepted but seen as an essential part of life. It is important to recognise that drug problems involve middle-aged and elderly people as well as young people. Young people may use different drugs but it is a fact that the middle-aged and elderly most use drugs. As they grow up in a drug-saturated society, it is not surprising that young people take drugs to solve problems; after all it is what they have seen and heard and learned to do. Often the drugs their elders use cause less worry and shock but that does not mean that they are less dangerous or less addictive. One of the most rampant epidemic of drug misuse and abuse has been that of sedative and tranquilliser drugs. Alcohol, Librium, Mogadon, Valium and sleep-inducing drugs are included in this category. Often it is forgotten that alcohol is also a drug of addiction and that it leads to more serious problems than all the illegal drugs put together. Most alcoholics are not young people but research shows us that a growing proportion of adolescents and young adults are now abusing alcohol.

Drugs are not all equally dangerous. However every drug can be abused, and even the commonest of drugs, for example paracetamol, can kill. But there are degrees of danger, and cannabis is not in the same league as heroin. Sometimes, however, the attention paid to a drug is not in proportion to its potentially harmful effects. For years the dangers of sleeping tablets and tranquilliser were passed over, while the horrors of 'pot'-smoking were loudly denounced. Alcohol is also a lethal drug and though the percentage of alcohol-users who become seriously affected is less than the percentage of heroin users who do so, the overall numbers involved are still higher for alcohol.

Many of the dangers for drug addicts lie as much in their lifestyle and their manner of using the drug as in the drug itself. Many drugs of addiction are important and powerful painkillers and can be used to great advantage, but heroin, for example, when sold on the street, is often so impure and adulterated with substances such as talcum powder or even cement that it becomes highly dangerous to life.

There is a current description of drugs as being 'hard' or 'soft'. For the most part this is misleading. Some drugs which can cause physical dependency and psychological harm are often termed 'soft', for example Valium. People often think that everyone who takes a certain type of illegal drug is addicted. Parents worry that if young people take cannabis that they will soon start to use a more dangerous drug such as heroin. The real picture is more complex. Most heroin addicts, although not all, have used cannabis, but not all cannabis-users progress to heroin. However becoming part of a drug culture, with drug-oriented companions and a lifestyle that revolves around drugs as an answer, escape and goal can often lead to experimentation with more dangerous types of drugs.

Different people are affected by a drug in different ways, and personality can be an integral part of the equation, as can environment and expectations. The World Health Organisation defines a drug as 'any substance that, when taken into the living organism, may modify one or more of its functions.'

We can identify and categorise some of these different substances. This may help us to understand better their relative potential for harm, both in the short term and the long term. Each drug has a particular effect on the individual and recognising the symptoms of a particular drug can be a warning signs of abuse.

Firstly there are some general signs of abuse of drugs:

- Loss of appetite
- Unusual sleepiness or inability to sleep
- Lethargy, lack of interest in hobbies or sports
- Changing friendship patterns
- Loss of interest in schoolwork
- Truancy
- Telling lies or acting secretively
- Money or valuables disappearing from home
- Unusually irritable, aggressive or even violent responses
- Coming to the notice of police for unruly, disorderly or dishonest behaviour
- Unusual spots, sores and marks on the body, arms or around the mouth and nose.

49

- Stains and chemical smells on clothing or around the body

TESSA

Tessa has shown many of the symptoms of drug abuse for quite a few months. Fred, her elder brother, has been challenging her about this and has ended up arguing with his parents about her. He is very sensitive to her disruptive and argumentative behaviour at home, her quarrelling with her younger sisters and more recently her abusive treatment of her mother. He knows her friends, and he knows they do drugs. He sees her constantly smoking and sneaking out of classes to meet them. She has been lying a lot about where she has been, and he has suspected her of stealing small change from his room. He knows his mother has been missing money also, although she tried to convince herself that she had been miscalculating.

Fred is only seventeen but is genuinely worried about his younger sister. At two years his junior, she has always been part of his 'crowd' and he has always looked out for her. But now she has changed, become uninterested in him and her old friends and even rude to them. He wonders where the Tessa he always knew has gone. He sees flashes of her—she can still be kindly—but she used to be a proper little Laura Ingalls, always doing nice things, like running the bath for you and putting her own bath foam into it or making you a cup of tea or tidying the house for mum. She always had a smile and she regularly arrived with sweets for the younger kids out of her own money. No wonder mum and dad couldn't face up to the changes in Tessa; they kept looking for the sweet-natured daughter and denying that she was gone. The last straw was when Tessa was brought home by a policeman. She had been found shoplifting in a local store. Tessa loudly denied it and had a lengthy explanation involving a friend, another bag, and a long queue at another check-out. Fred wondered if his parents would buy this latest fairytale or would they, like him, start looking at the full picture.

1 Inhalants or Solvents

When young people are abusing these substances they deliberately inhale gases, fumes or vapours to get a high or a buzz similar to the intoxication caused by alcohol. The term in general use is 'glue-sniffing', but this more accurately is known as 'volatile substance abuse' or 'solvent abuse'. Glue is not the only substance used, just one of a large number of readily available, relatively inexpensive and easily concealed solvents. Many household and industrial products can be abused and therefore are readily accessible to young people. It has been estimated that an average household has about thirty substances that can be abused, and new products are being found and experimented with all the time. They are often more readily available to young people than alcohol.

Substances abused
- Antifreeze
- Cigarette lighter fuel/Butane gas
- Petroleum products
- Dry-cleaning fluids
- Hair lacquer
- Gas canisters and bottles
- Nail varnish remover
- Surgical spirit
- Shoe polish
- Metal cleaners and polish dyes
- Shoe conditioners
- Room deodorants
- Paints
- Thinners
- Paint and plaster removers
- Typewriter correcting fluids and thinners (Tipp-X)
- Glues for model aeroplanes
- Cement contact adhesives
- Air fresheners
- Flu spray
- Paint spray
- Hair spray
- Fire extinguishers
- Painkilling spray

A volatile substance is one that is usually a liquid but will become a vapour or gas under normal conditions at room temperature. In a gaseous state a substance is absorbed through the lungs and into the bloodstream, in which it rapidly travels to the brain. Abusers inhale or sniff the product from a soaked rag, coat sleeve, handkerchief, cotton wool, pillow or from a bottle. Material is sometimes placed in a plastic or paper bag, for example a crisp bag and held over the face, nose or head. This concentrates the fumes.

Inhalants work by slowing down the body's functions much like an anaesthetic. Initially users feels slightly stimulated; they then lose inhibitions and control. Because the central nervous system also becomes anaesthetised breathing can become slow and difficult and judgement may be impaired. The users often appear 'drunk' and may stagger and appear uncoordinated. Nausea, coughing, sneezing, dizziness and lack of appetite are some of the rapid and unpleasant side-effects. Hallucinations ranging from mild and pleasurable to extremely frightening may also occur. Behaviour can become aggressive or even violent. Effects are short-lived, ranging from a few minutes to half an hour. Young people can thus often conceal their drug use, though a chemical smell may cling to them.

Volatile organic solvents produce more unwanted or toxic effects than do most other drugs. The effects are rapid because the substances enter the bloodstream through the lungs and often takes users by surprise. There may be a vacant stare or slurred speech. Sometimes users may lose consciousness and may even die if their breathing rate drops too low or if they inhale vomit or suffocate because of the plastic bag. Sudden death may result from the direct toxic effect of some solvents. Cardiac arrest may also occur. Even brief exposures can disrupt the normal functioning of the heart, sometimes causing death. Over an extended period inhalants can cause permanent damage to the central nervous system (including the brain), muscle fatigue, salt imbalance, cardiac irregularities, conjunctivitis, liver and kidney damage, adverse effects on blood and bone marrow, and a permanent 'sniffer's rash' around the nose and throat.

Initially abusers may sniff only occasionally, either alone or as part of a group. Many experimenters try solvent abuse once or twice, then stop. Sometimes their curiosity has been satisfied or they feel sick or their parents find out or their group is no longer interested. Boredom can be a major factor, and the element of risk-taking is very attractive to the young abusers. Sometimes, though, young people may become compulsive about use and may start to sniff or inhale on a regular, even daily basis. The body develops a tolerance to these drugs and this forces young people to use greater amounts, more frequently, to get high. If they lose the ability to stop sniffing they tend to hide their habit, often spending hours alone in an intoxicated state. Often no one is aware of the extent to which the drug use has become compulsive, not their friends nor even the young people themselves. These are the abusers who are most at risk. Their health is damaged, although heart, brain, kidneys and liver damage is usually seen only after several years' use. Accidents are a common cause of fatalities; falls, burns or drownings that occur when the young person is intoxicated, often alone. Insomnia and depression are also associated with long-term use.

Telltale signs
- Drunken behaviour
- Antisocial behaviour including violence, aggression and dishonesty
- Rowdy and silly behaviour, and uncontrollable giggling
- General decline in performance at school
- Truancy
- Change in personality or mental confusion
- Possession of plastic bags and solvents
- Glue or solvent stains on clothing
- Chemical smell on breath
- Red eyes or heightened facial colouring
- Unusual spots, marks or rings around the mouth or nose
- Persistent cough or runny nose

When young people have been using solvents they may suffer from a 'hangover' and have poor concentration. Withdrawal symptoms which may develop after regular use include sleep-disturbance, nausea, stomach cramps, general irritability and facial tics.

TOM
When he was about twelve, Tom abused solvents regularly. He would buy lighter gas or petrol, paint thinner or Tipp-X and meet his pals in the fields behind their estate. Mostly the abuse occurred at weekends, but Tom just lived for these occasions. He thought it was brilliant and felt a great sense of

escape and also of belonging. Between them, he and his mates could always manage to afford something to sniff. A couple of times he had flashbacks where he experienced hallucinations even though he wasn't using solvents, and this frightened him. It didn't stop him though. Around this time he started mitching from school and going up the fields with some petrol, even on his own. He often sniffed gas in school. One of his mates was caught with stuff by his father and the group of sniffers broke up. The friend didn't rat though, and Tom's parents never found out. His friend told his dad it was a once-off occasion. It was just coming into the summer and Tom was sent to his cousins down the country where he was introduced to alcohol.

ALICE AND NORA

Alice had been shocked by one of her friends. They went babysitting one night and Nora started to inhale some air-freshener that was in the kitchen. She couldn't understand why Alice wouldn't take any, and kept giggling and laughing and trying to coax Alice. To Alice it seemed disgusting, but Nora used a full can of air freshener quite quickly. ' It's fantastic,' she kept saying. Alice got frightened when Nora started to hit her and get angry with her for no reason. She seemed drunk and out of control but when the can was finished she soon quietened down and except for a headache later on seemed OK. A short while afterwards Nora was found unconscious in her bedroom and rushed to hospital. Though Alice couldn't know for sure that seemed to be the end of Nora's solvent abuse.

Amyl nitrite and butyl nitrite are also inhalants. They are known as 'poppers' snappers rush, locker room, nitrates or bananas. They are alleged to intensify sexual experiences and are often imported into the country as room deodorisers, in small brown bottles.

2. Cannabis

Cannabis is used by millions of people throughout the world and is the most widely abused illegal drug in the United Kingdom. It is a mild hallucinogen. The active mind-altering ingredient is THC (tetrahydrocannabinol). The amount of

THC determines how strong the effects will be. Cannabis comes from a large plant, called *cannabis sativa*, and has various forms:

- Marijuana (pot, grass, reefer): the leaves and fruiting tops of the plant
- Hashish (hash, blow): resin extracted from the hairs on the plant
- Hash oil: a concentrated extract

The amount of THC and its potency, varies according to where and how the plant was cultivated. Marijuana has 5–10 per cent THC, cannabis resin or hashish has up to 20 per cent and hash oil has a potency as high as 85 per cent.

Hashish comes in a variety of forms and colours, depending on country of origin. This leads to nicknames, for example Paki black or Lebanese gold or Afghan black. Commonly used slang names for cannabis in its various forms also include

- Grass, Hash, Charge
- Pot, Hay, Dagga
- Joint,Weed, Dope
- Smoke, Shit, Marijuana
- Blow, Stuff, Mary
- Reefer, Tea

The most common way of consuming cannabis is by smoking. A joint is made by rolling a cigarette using marijuana or herbal cannabis in place of, or with tobacco, or mixing cannabis resin or oil with tobacco. Cannabis smoke is very hot and can burn the throat, so often long joints, or filters, or pipes of various sizes are made. Cannabis can also be swallowed and is sometimes made into a tea-like drink or cooked in home made cakes and sweets. There can be an enormous variation in the amount of THC between one joint and another, up to 30,000 per cent.

The effects then obviously depend on the type and quantity used, also on the users' mood and expectations and the situation. Almost immediately after intake, the heart beats faster, pulse rate quickens, and mouth and throat gets drier. There are likely to be pleasurable feelings of elation, gaiety and well-being. Cannabis removes inhibitions and the user becomes very excitable, talkative and relaxed. Some people have trouble remembering events that occurred during the high and experience difficulty in performing functions that require concentration, rapid reactions and coordination, like driving. Reflexes are slowed and judgement impaired even up to six hours after using. Mixing alcohol with cannabis causes performance to deteriorate further.

Acute intoxication can result in anxiety, paranoia and panic. Sometimes users become aggressive, even violent. Once the drug wears off, there may be a 'hangover' of headache, nausea and general disability and fatigue. Regular smoking causes sleep-loss or disturbance, irritability and restlessness, decreased appetite, sweating, weight loss and depression. Cannabis unlike alcohol is not water soluble, so it accumulates in the body-fat, tissues and organs, leading to build up of THC.

Cannabis smoke contains approximately 2,000 chemicals and has a quicker and more damaging effect on the lungs than tobacco. The risk of lung cancer is greater. The amount of carcinogen retained after one joint of cannabis is probably greater than that from five normal tobacco cigarettes, because cannabis smoke is inhaled deeply and held for as long as thirty seconds. Two to three joints a day may carry the same risk of lung damage as a pack of cigarettes. Cannabis can also cause emphysema. THC reduces the body's capacity to resist infectious diseases. Evidence also exists that cannabis negatively affects the human reproductive system, causing irregular menstrual cycles in women and temporary loss of fertility in men. It has also been shown to influence the levels of some hormones related to sexuality. Because adolescence is a time of sexual development and maturation, young people are at high risk of damage to their sexual functioning and hormone bchrisce. Cannabis can also cause low birth weight and premature babies.

Cannabis is often used with other drugs and this interaction can cause fatal overdoses, since it prolongs or exaggerates the effect on the central nervous system of depressants such as alcohol. Cannabis alters the effect of many other drugs, for example alcohol, amphetamines, cocaine, opiates, nicotine, benzodiazepines and barbiturates.

Young people are also at high risk when they use cannabis because of its tendency to cause lethargy and lack of interest in school work and hobbies. It impairs memory and learning ability, can interfere with verbal and mathematical skills and the ability to think clearly and read with comprehension. The extended use of cannabis can lead to 'burn-out'—where a user can become dull, slow-moving and inattentive. Some individuals as young as sixteen may suffer 'burn-out'.

RAY

Ray at sixteen is totally in denial that cannabis can ever cause him harm. Already he feels that he cannot get to sleep at night without a smoke and he will stop at practically nothing to make sure that he has some 'blow' to get him through the day. His friends notice that his voice is slurred and that he is very 'dopey' but mostly they go along with the view that hash is OK, just a smoke after all. They do not realise the potential physical consequences for Ray or themselves and that cannabis is psychologically addictive. Though cannabis use does not automatically lead to abuse of other drugs, the reliance on a chemical to change moods or feelings and the move into a specific drug culture leave young people more at risk of experimenting with and developing further drug relationships.

3 Depressants/Sedatives

Depressants are drugs which calm you down or send you to sleep by depressing the central nervous system (which includes the brain). They are also known as sedatives or hypnotics. Hypnotics are drugs that induce sleep. Depressants are used to treat stress, anxiety, sleeplessness, mental disorders and some cases of epilepsy. They have a high potential for abuse and are frequently known as 'downers'. Tranquillisers, barbiturates, benzodiazepines and alcohol all belong to this group.

Barbiturates

These come as tablets or capsules in various sizes and colours. They all depress the central nervous system, but effect, duration and toxicity may vary. Long-acting barbiturates produce sleep that can last up to ten hours. They build up in the body and result in a 'hangover' which is dangerous as it can impair skill and concentration. There is a fine line between the dosage that produces sleep and that which kills.

The prescribing of barbiturates is now discouraged and so they find their way on to the black market. They include Amytal, sometimes known as Lilly; Soneryl, Seconal and Tuinal. Street names include birds, blue heavens, reds, sleepers, red devils, rainbows, barbs, angels, candy, goofballs, downers.

Misusers feel relieved of worry and tension. They act unpredictably or show signs of mental confusion, though some look happy and relaxed. Even in small doses, barbiturates caused slurred speech, staggering walk, poor judgement and reflexes. Users frequently lose their balance and fall.

Benzodiazepines

There are major tranquillisers and minor tranquillisers. Major tranquillisers are used to treat severe mental illness and do not produce physical dependence. It is the minor tranquillisers and hypnotics (or sleep-inducing drugs) which come mainly from a group of drugs called benzodiazepines and which are often abused. They are used to treat restlessness, depression, tension and anxiety, that is to tranquillise or sedate; as sleeping tablets for insomnia; as muscle relaxants; and for other medical purposes. Benzodiazepines are not easily recognisable by their shape and colour because there are so many different manufacturers. This means that a user can be easily mistaken as to type and dosage unless the drugs are specifically prescribed for them. Both tranquillisers and hypnotics vary in terms of the duration of their effects. Some last only a few hours while others have a more prolonged effect, lasting even into the next day. There are even greater hazards involved when young people steal, buy or simply accept offered tablets.

Common names of benzodiazepines:
- Ativan
- Rohypnol
- Librium
- Normison
- Valium

- Dalmane
- Nobrium
- Roche Mogadon
- Roche Serenid
- Xanax
- Tranxene
- Halcion

These drugs became immensely popular, indicating that a great many people felt the need for such medication, or their doctors did. However they have caused great concern because a large portion of the population are needlessly and harmfully placing a chemical barrier between themselves and the stresses, strains and, yes, anxieties of life. Minor tranquillisers can be dangerous even when taken as directed, especially when taken for a long period. When individuals try to stop after long-term usage, withdrawal causes jitteriness, panic attacks, loss of appetite and body weight, nausea, strange tastes and smells, tremors, perspiration and even convulsions.

These symptoms reflect the fact that the individual has developed physical dependency on the drugs. This is not the same as being addicted. Dependence on benzodiazepines can develop even in people who take the relatively small doses that have been prescribed by their doctors. This physical dependency can be described as a physiological change occurring due to taking the drugs. The abuse of a drug, on the other hand, or craving for a drug is usually symptomised by drug-seeking behaviour, for example buying from drug dealers, conning prescriptions from several doctors or altering a prescription so that larger amounts can be obtained. Not every one who uses drugs of abuse is a drug abuser, just as not everyone who drinks alcohol is an alcoholic. The young people who abuse tranquillisers, sedatives and hypnotics are usually those who have already abused other drugs, for example, alcohol, barbiturates or opiates. Research in the US has indicated that these drugs are used recreationally by teenagers, many of them (approximately 20 million in US at the time of survey), school students having used them on at least twenty occasions. Girls are more likely than boys to use tranquillisers.

One thing is clear, however: young people do abuse benzodiazepines, often in conjunction with alcohol. Often there are supplies in their own home, perhaps forgotten about, and parents are often not aware of the danger of misuse. The euphoric effect of these drugs is enhanced when they are used with alcohol. The danger of overdose is very real when young people take benzodiazapines with alcohol. It is not at all difficult to die from a combination of, for example, Valium and alcohol. Even a small amount of alcohol can produce intoxication in someone who has taken a single Valium tablet. Often young people already addicted to analgesics or opiates will abuse them. Sometimes young people inject benzodiazepines using the gel or liquid in the capsules, with all the attendant dangers of injecting.

KEITH

Keith uses Rohypnol and Dalmane to spike up his high from alcohol. He gets them quite easily from dealers. Initially he stole them from his grandparents, who both find sleeping difficult. When he called to them it was very easy to go to the bathroom cabinet and sneak a few. Later he got greedy and took a whole bottle. Neither of them said anything but from that point there were no sleeping tablets in the cabinet. Keith has started abusing many other drugs in his search for constant oblivion. He is also abusing opiates.

Research probing the question of why young people take drugs has shown that fathers are likely to drink alcohol (though not necessarily heavily) while mothers are likely to be users of prescription drugs, for example tranquillisers. The key issue here is that young people are growing up in an environment where drug taking (albeit legal) is accepted as part and parcel of everyday life.

Telltale Signs
- Slurred speech
- Slow, unsteady reflexes
- Poor judgement
- Acting intoxicated, with no odour on breath
- Tendency to fall asleep even in unusual situations
- Listlessness, lack of energy
- Lack of interest in school work and hobbies

Alcohol

One of the basic facts about alcohol that young people (or many people of any age) fail to grasp is that it is a drug. It is a sedative; that is, it puts you to sleep. Ethyl alcohol was the first of the sedatives to be discovered and is easily available in our culture without prescription. It is the only drug which is absorbed in significant quantities through the stomach and thus it reaches the bloodstream faster than most other sedatives. An individual can get rid of alcohol from the body only at the rate of one drink every hour, that is, one 12 oz-can of beer; one glass of wine; one small sherry; one pub measure of spirits. No matter how much he drinks all the alcohol is gone from the body within twenty-four hours after his last drink.

When the blood alcohol level goes up, something happens in the brain. Ethyl alcohol depresses the various centres in the brain. Like all sedatives, it diminishes or stops normal functioning. It works first on the cerebrum, which controls intellectual and rational thought and judgement, then on the spinal cord, then on the vital centres, for example breathing and the heart. Alcohol first leaves you confused, then unable to walk, then unconscious with no reflexes, then dead.

Alcohol has two effects:

- It diminishes psychomotor activity, leaving the individual relaxed, less anxious, less worried than before.
- It increases psychomotor activity.

Because of the first effect, the second effect is not immediately experienced. The first effect lasts for two to three hours and starts to decrease as blood-alcohol levels start to fall. The second effect lasts for about twelve hours. This means that you can't take a drink without an agitating effect that wears off slowly so that you end up more tense than you began. This is why we often end up having another drink and also why the cure for a hangover is said to be 'a hair of the dog'. We are again trying to sedate this agitation with alcohol. If someone has been drinking very heavily it may take days for his or her psychomotor activity to return to normal. He or she will be anxious, shaking, sweating, restless. Sometimes this occurs even while the individuals are still drinking: they have increased the second effect to such a degree that alcohol can no longer sedate them. This accounts for hangovers, withdrawal symptoms and eventually *delirium tremens* (DTs) where the individual is so agitated and anxious that he is in a state of terror and may even get convulsions, depending on much has been drunk and for how long.

When you drink alcohol, not all the effects are reversible. Brain cells, once destroyed, cannot regenerate themselves. Fortunately, we have many more brain cells than we need as we are probably losing some every day. If you lose 10 per cent of your brain, no one might notice, but if you lose 20 to 30 per cent even you might become aware that you cannot think through a problem or remember as well as you used to. When enough of the brain is damaged, there are irreversible changes in a person's behaviour and psychological status. He or she may never return to normal. Even moderate levels of alcohol impairs learning and memory capabilities. Obviously this has important implications for young people who are drinking regularly and who sometimes have alcohol in their system from the day before, affecting their skill, memory, attention, reflexes and judgement. One of the signs of addiction is when tolerance is increased. A young person may pride himself on being able to drink his friends under the table without realising he is damaging his brain and other cells at a rapid rate.

- Among the group of sedative drugs, one can replace the other at any time. The effect on the brain is almost identical, depending on dosage. This means that there is cross-dependency or tolerance within this group. If someone is physically dependent on one, for example a tranquilliser, he or she can substitute with another sedative, like alcohol.
- Obviously if someone is an alcoholic and comes off alcohol only to go on another sedative he is not dealing with a dependency, simply substituting one for another. This cross-tolerance, which feeds into cross-addiction, also accounts for the fact that it takes a larger amount of anaesthetic to knock someone out if he is alcoholic, as all anaesthetists know.
- Sometimes when people drink they can be walking around, talking, even driving a car and yet the next day they will not remember it. This is called a blackout. There is a considerable amount of dysfunction in a brain that blacks

out.

- Alcohol also affects the stomach. It is an irritant and causes loss of appetite, disturbed digestion, impaired absorption and vomiting. Vomiting is an all too familiar occurrence when young people drink, especially when experimenting.
- Heartburn is often experienced as a result of drinking on an empty stomach because of irritation to the lining. This can lead to ulcers or chronic inflammation of the stomach lining called gastritis. Cancer of the stomach and colon is a long-term risk.
- Most alcohol passes through the liver on its way to the bloodstream, and it here that alcohol is metabolised or broken down into safer components. In cases of excessive drinking, fat accumulates in the liver, impairing functioning, and where there is consistent damage, cirrhosis of the liver occurs with parts of the liver dying and being replaced by scar tissue. We cannot function entirely without our liver to deal with toxins in our body but when the liver is damaged we can operate with only part of it. The difficulty is that when a certain point is passed, and too much liver is damaged, there is no going back.
- Alcohol also increases the volume of urine because of the effect on the pituitary gland.
- Heavy alcohol use is a leading cause of heart disease and circulatory disorders as large quantities of alcohol make the heart 'fatty' and weak.
- A dangerous effect of alcohol for young people is that it increases the flow in blood vessels near the skin. Because there is more blood, people feels warm, but they are actually losing heat. Often young people drink in the open, sleeping where they are sitting, and this leads to the danger of hypothermia.
- One of the greatest causes of death in young people is accidents occurring when they have been drinking. For this reason alone, alcohol is more dangerous than all other drugs put together. When you drink, initially inhibitions are removed, but attention and judgement are impaired, as are self-discipline and skills involving fine coordination. Your ability to see clearly is affected, as is your capacity to recognise colour differences. Later there is confusion, errors

in coordination, loss of balance. This means a person is at risk. Young people are notoriously unable to recognise their limits, often thinking they are invincible even without alcohol. Alcohol frequently leads them to misjudge danger and take risks which can lead to loss of life, particularly, but not only, when driving.

- When young people drink they often mix the alcohol with other sedatives like tranquillisers, cold and cough remedies and allergy medications. This is more than doubling the danger. Violence, arrests, falls, drownings, road accidents all are more likely when someone is drinking.

TOM

When Tom goes out drinking, he usually gets into trouble. He insults people; he won't pay his share; he walks down the middle of busy roads. He fights with others and feels no pain. He doesn't know his own strength and has been known to climb scaffolding on building sites and walk on high walls. He gets into cars with others who are also drunk (sometimes stolen cars) and they drive at 100 m.p.h.

Blood alcohol level

Young people under eighteen should be encouraged not to drink but since there is a high probability that they will drink anyway they should know that intoxication or drunkenness depends on your blood alcohol level. This depends on:

- Your sex: if you are female, it takes less to get you drunk because you have more fatty tissue than a male and this does not absorb as much alcohol.
- Your weight and build: the heavier you are, the lower the concentration of alcohol in the blood.
- The type of drink: spirits are absorbed more quickly than beer or wine.
- How quickly you drink: slow yourself down. Take a mineral between drinks. Have a spritzer rather than a glass of wine.
- When you last ate: food in the stomach delays the absorption of alcohol. Remember it doesn't stop it. Lining your stomach doesn't mean you can drink more.
- How much you drink: remember your body can only deal with one drink in one hour. Any more accumulates in your

body. Avoid rounds of drink.

- Your mood: if you are drinking to deal with feelings you are more at risk. Avoid drinking when you are depressed, nervous or angry, as this is the sort of drinking that is more likely to become addictive.
- Your pattern of drinking: if you are drinking constantly or every day this affects how your body copes with alcohol.

You are never too young to have problems with alcohol. Often young people think:

- You can't become an alcoholic when you're young
- You can't become alcoholic if you don't drink alone
- You can't become alcoholic if you don't drink every day.
- You can't become alcoholic if you don't get into trouble or fights
  These are all untrue.

There are some questions you can ask yourself if you or someone else is worried about your drinking:

- Do you drink because you have problems or to help you face up to stressful situations?
- Do you drink because it's 'cool' to be able to hold your drink?
- Do you ever drink in the morning before school or work?
- Do you ever drink alone rather than with others?
- Do you drink in gulps as if to satisfy a great thirst?
- Do you drink when you get cross with other people, your parents, teachers, friends?
- When you drink do you often get drunk, even if you don't intend to?
- Do you ever find it hard to remember what you did at the time you were drinking?
- When you drink do you ever get into trouble of any kind?
- Does drinking ever lead you to be dishonest with yourself or with others about how much you drink?
- Does your drinking ever affect your performance at school, college or work?
- Has your drinking led you to try unsuccessfully to stop or to drink less?

If you can answer *yes* to any one of these questions, it's

probably time you took a serious look at what your drinking might be doing to you. Nobody is too young to have trouble with alcohol. The more you drink, the more likely you are to become dependent on it.

4 Stimulants

These drugs stimulate the central nervous system and are called uppers because they produce almost immediate strength and energy.

There are mild socially acceptable stimulants such as caffeine which are not often thought of as drugs. Caffeine is contained in coffee, tea, Coke and Lucozade. Many people are dependent on caffeine, unable to get through the day without their 'fix', mild though the dose may seem. Nicotine is also a stimulant.

Cocaine is probably one of the best known and most powerful of stimulants. Ecstasy is also part-stimulant. Stimulants produce euphoria, excitement and increased activity and the user can go without sleep for long periods. Serious psychological dependency can easily develop because of the euphoria and pleasurable feelings involved.

Cocaine

Cocaine is sometimes known as the 'champagne of drugs'. For centuries the leaves of the cocoa plant have been chewed by South American Indians. They seldom contained more than 2 per cent cocaine, but about 100 years ago a technique was developed to extract cocaine hydrochloride and the use of cocaine soon spread far and wide.

It is bitter-tasting white crystalline powder, giving rise to such names as 'snow' and 'white lady'. When it is sold on the street it can be adulterated by any one of numerous cutting agents, the product ending up at anything from 30 to 60 per cent cocaine hydrochloride. Usually these agents are lactose or mannitol, a local anaesthetic which gives a similar localised anaesthesia to cocaine. However, the cocaine is sometimes adulterated with dangerous substances such as rat poison. This powder is snorted or sniffed, or injected. Usually a small quantity is placed on a mirror, chopped into a fine powder and put into a 'line' with a razor blade. This is then sniffed into the nostrils through a straw, tube or rolled banknote.

Prolonged sniffing can cause ulceration and perforation of the nasal sputum. Some addicts are left severely disfigured by this. When cocaine is injected it destroys the skin tissues and causes ulcers. Traditional cocaine powders are cocaine hydrochloride, cocaine sulfate and cocaine base.

Cocaine hydrochloride is also neutralised to either 'freebase' or 'crack'. These forms of cocaine can be smoked. Crack comes in the form of a yellow, rocky lump of white granules like marble. It is known as 'rock', 'wash' or 'flake'. Crack is usually smoked with a water pipe. Homemade varieties are devised from soft drink cans, plastic and glass bottles, glass tubing, drinking glasses and tinfoil. The drug is heated gently. This in known as 'freebasing'.

Cocaine brings with it a feeling of exhilaration, well-being and euphoria, which can be followed by agitation. The vaso-constrictive properties of cocaine actually diminish the possibility of absorption through the nasal tissues as the user continues to inhale. On the other hand, when cocaine is smoked as freebase or crack, the self-limiting property is lost as the drug is absorbed directly into the lungs. Also, street cocaine is usually only 15 to 25 per cent pure, while crack can be 90 per cent pure. This means that the drug reaches the brain in a more concentrated form. Crack has a short, intense high, produced in four to six seconds with the euphoria lasting only five to six minutes. This intense euphoria is the hook which leads to psychological dependency.

When cocaine is snorted or sniffed an effect occurs within one to three minutes and lasts up to half an hour. Cocaine's ability to produce a sense of power and exhilaration is followed by a deep depression. This pattern almost guarantees addiction. As users come down they feel depressed, lose energy and appetite, have difficulty sleeping and feel horrible about themselves.

Physical effects of cocaine
Long-term cocaine users lose weight, develop skin problems (such as facial dermatitis, drying, peeling), experience convulsions, have difficulty breathing and often spit up black phlegm. Long-term snorting can ulcerate the mucous membrane of the nose. Smoking cocaine can lead to emphysema. Cocaine slows digestion, masks hunger,

stimulates the central nervous system and induces agitation, restlessness, apprehensiveness and sexual arousal. Its immediate effects are elevated blood pressure, temperature, pulse, blood sugar and breathing rate. This can lead to cardio-vascular problems such as elevated heart and blood pressure, tachyarrhythmia and heart attack, cerebral haemorrhage and even death. When it is injected, disease results from dirty needles.

Cocaine users commonly complain about anxiety, memory lapses and depression. They may have feelings of restlessness, sleeplessness, irritability, loss of sexual desire, violent behaviour, chronic cough and sometimes hallucinations of touch, sight, taste or smell (cocaine psychosis).

Paranoia is another frequent result of abuse. There is no safe dose of cocaine. Users can also get a sensation like insects crawling over their skin (cocaine bugs) or visual disturbances (snow lights). Freebasing has a shorter more intense high but has increased risks, including confusion, slurred speech and anxiety.

Tell-tale signs
- Tremors
- Hyperactivity (when using)
- Insomnia
- Dilated pupils
- Euphoria
- Lack of energy
- Depression
- Oversleeping
- Overeating (when in withdrawal)
- Inability to concentrate
- Irritability
- Restlessness

PATRICK

When Patrick goes out on a Friday night he has two main aims. One is to deal drugs, usually wraps of cocaine (small amounts in folded pieces of paper) cannabis and Ecstasy. He has a couple of girls also selling Ecstasy (E) for him. He gives them each a plastic bag of about 200 tablets which they conceal in their bra or knickers, knowing that the police are less likely to question them than a boy. Patrick deals at a higher level because he needs more to feed his own habit. Patrick is into cannabis and cocaine.

Caffeine

This is the most widely used drug worldwide. It is found in coffee, tea, cola drinks, in some tonics and many painkilling tablets. A similar drug is found in cocoa (drinking chocolate) and chocolate.

Five to six cups of tea gives approximately 270 mgs of caffeine. One cup of freshly brewed coffee gives 100–150 mgs of caffeine. Instant coffee give 70 mgs of caffeine, Cola gives 15–55 mgs of caffeine per can. Headache tablets give approximately 50 mgs per tablet.

Half an hour after those two cups of coffee you begin to feel your high. Your metabolism, temperature and blood pressure increase, as does your blood sugar level. Tolerance to caffeine builds up. Even if you only take four cups of coffee per days you crave your cup of coffee, feel you need it to face the day, begin to need more and more. When people use coffee continuously or extensively, they may experience hand tremors, loss of appetite, poor co-ordination and delayed or difficult sleep. Extensive use of extremely high doses of caffeine may cause nausea, diarrhoea, trembling, headache, nervousness and sleeplessness. Poisonous doses lead to convulsions, though these and death can only occur through use of tablets. (10g caffeine is the lethal dose).

Nicotine

Nicotine is one of the most toxic of all poisons. It enters the body through the lungs (when smoked), through the mouth (when chewed), or through the stomach and intestines (when swallowed). It is habit-forming and psychologically addictive. The user craves nicotine practically constantly and high tolerance builds up quickly. It leads to loss of appetite, restlessness and irritability. Nicotine has been associated with many health problems such as cancer, and cardiovascular and respiratory diseases. Smokeless tobacco, for example gum or dried wads, increases the risk of cancer of the gum and mouth by 5000 per cent.

Amphetamines and Ecstasy

The most common home-made amphetamine is amphetamine

sulphate, which is found in tablets, loose powder with a selection of colours, and textures and capsules. It is bulked up with whole range of substances ranging from lactose to caffeine to paracetamol. It is easily produced and readily available on the street, being known widely as 'speed'. The purity of drugs at street level is extremely low, about 6 per cent. Speed can be swallowed, injected, smoked or snorted. Sometimes it is dissolved in a drink, rubbed on gums or sucked from a finger. The 'buzz' or 'rush' produces an overwhelming sense of euphoria, happiness, 'being in heaven'. There may also be nervous excitability, sleeplessness, agitation, talkativeness, aggressiveness, lack of appetite, unlimited energy, dry mouth and thirst, sweating, palpitations, increased blood pressure, nausea, sickness, headaches, dizziness, tremors.

The effects usually wear off in three to four hours when the user becomes tired, irritable depressed, and unable to concentrate. Often there are feelings of confusion, persecution, even violence.

Amphetamines are closely related to Ecstasy and have many similar effects. There is a strong desire to continue using amphetamine sulphate with a need to use increasing amounts. Most young people find that speed is as easily available as cigarettes, from young dealers they know, and in any of the discos they attend. This is Chris's favourite rush.

Telltale signs
- Hyperactivity
- Talkativeness
- Dilated pupils
- Insomnia

Dexedrine
Known as 'dexies', these are white-scored tablets made from another amphetamine salt. Methylamphetamine is a similar amphetamine in appearance but is much more potent. It is known to give a 'better high' and is associated with bizarre and violent behaviour. During 1987 a new form became available, known as 'ice', 'glass' or 'ice-cream' which gives an intense 'rush' with a euphoria lasting from two to sixteen hours. This has many adverse side-effects: fever and nausea, increased blood pressure, paranoid delusions, auditory hallu-

cinations, bizarre and aggressive behaviour.

Overdose of ice leads to convulsions, coma and death. Fatalities can occur after only small doses. Like cocaine there is no safe dose.

Ephedrine

This is often sold as amphetamine as it looks similar and acts in the same way on the central nervous system. Ice is made from this also.

Ritalin

This is a white-scored tablet which is prescribed for rarcolepsy, fatigue associated with depression, and for hyperactive children. It causes amphetamine-like dependency. Pemoline and Volatile are other tablets which are amphetamine-like drugs with similar effects.

Slimming tablets

These are prescribed for the obese and are abused regularly. They also stimulate the central nervous system;

Tenuate Dospan: white elongated tablets marked 'merrell'.

Duromine: grey/green or maroon/grey capsules.

Teronac: white tablets

Preludin, Ponderax: clear and blue capsules.

These have similar effects to amphetamines.

Methylenedioxymethylamphetamine (MDMA) or Ecstasy

This is a drug which is related to amphetamine and mescaline, with both stimulant and hallucinogenic properties. It is decribed as a psychedelic drug. It was originally designed in 1914 by a German drug company as an appetite suppressant. This potentially lethal drug is at the centre of the latest drug epidemic. It is very much associated with the newest drug culture, the rave scene. This is based around large discos or dance-clubs where repetitive and hypnotic dance music is played for hours without a break. Part of the attraction of Ecstasy for young people is the fact that it gives them the stamina, to dance for hours. It has been described as being 'like heaven, you love everyone', and 'like electrical charges running through your body'. The ravers have their own fashion, language, music. The craving for the drug and

71

high is very much part of the excitement of the whole scene.

Ecstasy is available in tablets and capsules of every colour and size. New forms are being manufactured and appearing on the street every day. Amphetamines, cocaine, heroin and LSD are often mixed in a cocktail with E, as it is known, within capsules. Sometimes these are sold as Ecstasy. The effect of the tablets, the 'buzz', varies from tablet to tablet, capsule to capsule and often dealers themselves do not know what they are selling. Embalming fluids, rat poison, detergent can all be contained within the cocktail. For this reason young people in the know will buy only from 'friends' and will not buy capsules.

Many of the young users of this drug do not care what they are using, so eager are they to get high and get into the scene. They buy it up on their way into the clubs and use it quickly because thirty minutes to one hour elapses before the dose takes effect. Because the 'buzz' is not immediate, some young people will think it's not working, or not as potent as they hope, and take further doses. Also young boys will dare each other to take higher and higher doses. This is extremely dangerous and can have fatal consequences. However most of the deaths so far seem to be associated with no more than one or two tablets. Here again is another drug where there is no safe dosage.

When young people take Ecstasy, they may initially experience an amphetamine-like 'rush' of euphoria, followed by several hours of peacefulness and heightened sensual awareness. The drug is said to improve communication between friends, increasing self- esteem and self-confidence. Inhibitions disappear. It is easy to see why it is so attractive to young people; no wonder it can appear 'like heaven'. Here they think they have found a place to belong, where they have love, confidence, togetherness and superhuman strength and energy.

Also in evidence are the other effects of stimulation of the central nervous system: excitement, increased activity and feeling wide awake. The pupils dilate and the mouth may go dry. Of concern is the effect on the heart which can become overstimulated, increasing blood pressure and the heart rate. There can be tightening of the jaw, feelings of nausea, dizziness and lack of coordination.

One frightening aspect of Ecstasy use is that, as with LSD, the young person may undergo flashback of the experience. This is where they have similar feelings, hear and see things long after they have stopped using the drug. This is particularly likely to happen when they have used Ecstasy for a prolonged period. The high is followed by exhaustion, anxiety, and depression which may last several days.

Deaths have been attributed to Ecstasy. Respiratory distress, heart failure, kidney failure and internal bleeding can all occur. Dehydration and exhaustion are other causes of fatalities, also stroke. Ecstasy causes calcium deficiency, crumbling teeth, receding gums, brittle bone disease. It has been linked with infertility, brain damage, and psychological disorders.

Some street names of Ecstasy:
- Love Doves
- California sunrise
- Grey sparkles
- Big brown ones
- Burgers
- Yellow submarines
- New Yorkers
- Dennis the Menace

TESSA

Tessa lives for her weekends. Her boyfriend Frank and she go to the raves on Friday and Saturday nights. Sometimes they buy some tabs for their own use on Sunday. When she talks about the raves you can see the excitement in her face and in her gestures. She sits up and her face lights up. Most of her friends go to the dance-clubs, scorning what they term the 'Yuppie' drinkers who are heading for the pubs. They stock up first by eating melon and banana. This is their way of protecting themselves. They dress up for the occasion and look forward to the sounds, smells and familiar faces.

'I never buy from anyone but my friends,' she says. 'That way I know what I'm getting. Ecstasy can be dangerous because they can sell you all sorts all sorts of things mixed up with it; they can sell you mixtures or "mad bastards". They're horse stimulants and drive you crazy. Once they were selling worm tablets. I saw a guy completely bloat up with E. I think he got a bad capsule. Another guy took too many and he was jerking and his eyes were rolling in his head. He went purple and red and an ambulance had to be called. You get it cheaper anyway if you know the dealer. Everyone knows a dealer; they're the same age or just older than us. A lot of people deal; it's a good way to keep yourself in drugs. I've been asked several times to take tablets of E to sell but Frank won't let me. It's normally £25 a tablet, but if they know you to see it's just £20. If you're on speaking terms it's £15 and a good friend gets them for £10. If you're a very good friend you can sometimes get it on the slate, that's for nothing, or on tab, that's to pay the next time. There's all different sorts of tablets and different ones give you a different "buzz".

'When you take E first you start to feel sick and wobbly and might even vomit. If you don't feel that you probably haven't got E. Sometimes you "scag out"! That's when you sit down and your legs start to jump and when you talk it's like you're on gear (heroin), all slow and drawn-out. Sometimes you can get a dance buzz where you get out there on the floor and the music goes through you. You feel like you're part of everything and you don't need anyone. You feel like you could go on for ever. You have to remember, though, to keep drinking. You can buy wine or drink water. I always ask the barmen for ice cubes. You can get a bad "buzz" too. Your muscles go all tight and tense and you feel always, really bad. You start to freak and think everything is against you and people are watching you or someone is out to get you. Yeah, you can get real paranoid sometimes. Another thing, you could be talking away and there'd be no one there.

'My favourite are the white tablets, Love Doves. Sometimes people think they're buying them and they get something else. They've got a dove on them. They make you feel happy, like you love everyone. It doesn't matter if it's a girl or your boyfriend or even if you've just met them. You can sit down and just talk your heart out about anything. You're totally uninhibited. But it depends, too, on your mood. Sometimes Frank and I get them just for ourselves. The brown ones can make you feel confused, you just don't know what to do. The buzz goes on for a long time. When you're at the dance-clubs you can get lots of other drugs too.

'One guy I know has his own recipe. He goes drinking first and then takes some Rohypnol to spice it up. He can also get E on slate and then maybe he'll do coke as well on slate. He sometimes takes Valium. But he always takes speed. He might take poppers and smoke some gear. At the end of the night he has to get Roche to help him sleep. He's not the only one who does that.

'I hate the next morning though. You want to stay in bed you feel so exhausted. You get a grinding headache and your jaws hurt so much you can't eat. All your muscles feel sore. Most of the people there are from fifteen to twenty-one. At about twenty or twenty-one they begin to stop. It's hard, though. I tried it for a while but it felt like there was nothing to do on a Friday night. I kept longing to go out. Drinking didn't seem like much fun. I kept thinking of everyone and imagining what was happening. My friend says the longing goes eventually. She wouldn't go back because she had started hearing things like voices, in the middle of the night. It's not doing that for me; I just love it. After all, it's not like I'm a junkie.'

FRANK

Frank has been around the scene longer than Tessa. He is nineteen and considers himself an old hand. He looks on the beginners to the scene with amusement. 'In the beginning they don't know what to do but you need to get to know the right people. When you've been doing E for a while you start to take more. I know guys who take up to fifteen tablets but it's no good to them. They don't even dance, just sit there. Once you use more, there's no going back; less E just doesn't do anything for you any more. It doesn't matter how long you stay away; you still need the amount you used before. You take some going into the rave, while you're there and when it is over. You're not going to sleep anyway once you use E. You go to someone's house or you just sit in the park. You don't feel the cold or the rain anyway. Sometimes you just keep walking. You could walk all over the city but you don't feel tired even if you've been dancing for hours. You might smoke hash to bring yourself down. Or Roche sleeping tablets to help you sleep.

'The effects don't wear off until the next day. You look

waxy, your face is sucked in because of all the sweat you lost and you can't talk properly to anyone because you can't eat. I haven't eaten Sunday dinner in months. Your pupils are still so black you can hardly see the colour. The downers are awful but they become a habit. In the beginning you feel like hanging yourself but you get used to them. I like to take two and two myself. Two Ecstasy and two acid in the night.'

Telltale signs
- Dilated Pupils
- Exhaustion
- Headaches
- Change of friends and scene
- Not wanting to get up in the morning
- Loss of appetite
- Restlessness

5 Hallucinogens

These drugs work directly on the brain. They cause a 'trip' involving changes in the perception of time and space which results in unreal sensations, the appearance of visions, the hearing of voices and delusions. The effects of hallucinogens depend in particular on the mood and mental attitude of the user, and the environment in which they are taken. The mental effects may be completely different every time, with changes of mood ranging from ecstatic joy to feelings of persecution and panic.

LSD (Lysergic Acid Diethylamide)
It is an extremely potent drug and minute quantities are formed into very small tablets or microdots and absorbed onto blotting paper, peel-off stars or cartoon figures. The strength is unpredictable. Young people buy a square at anything from £10 to £300.

Slang names
- Acid
- Blotters
- Mellow
- Tab

Some 'designer' names are:

- Batman
- Smiley
- Strawberry
- Double Dip Strawberry (Extra Strong)

The effects of LSD begin within an hour, build up for two to eight hours and slowly fade after about 12 hours. Physical effects are less important than mental and emotional effects and include increased heart rate and blood pressure, widening of pupils and rise in temperature. The ration of 'bad', unpleasant and frightening trips to pleasant effects seems to be high. These involve loss of emotional control, disorientation, depression, dizziness, panic and extreme fear. Often users feel they are being attacked and can resort to extreme violence. They may also feel invincible and try to walk on water or climb great heights. Fatalities have occurred when young people do such things while hallucinating. After a trip they may suffer anxiety or depression. 'Flashback' of the experience may occur weeks or months later. There are psychological dangers as psychoses can occur. Tolerance to LSD develops rapidly so that it takes much larger doses to achieve the same effects.

FRANK

Frank is also an 'expert' on LSD. 'We usually take acid together in a group, you know to support each other. You take half a square or a square and you just wait. I had a trip once out in the country. It is just fantastic. I could see all the colours in the grass and trees, one by one. I mean I could see them all; they were shining out at me, getting brighter and brighter. There were birds singing and I could see the sound and hear the colours all at once. I was under a tree and I became part of the tree and I was so happy but I began to realise that the other trees were after me and that they were looking at me and stretching their arms out at me. But I couldn't run away because I was a tree and I was rooted there and their branches were slowly, slowly, slowly moving nearer and I knew that if they got me they would slowly choke me to death. I was absolutely terrified. It went on and on and on. It was literally hours. My friends said I was frozen rock-hard, staring ahead. Even when you come out of the trip eventually it takes hours to be all right. You can know what people are thinking and you get very sensitive and think your friends don't want you or are talking about you.

Magic mushrooms

These grow in the fields locally and contain psilocybin, a hallucinogenic drug. Frank and Tessa have experimented with magic mushrooms. 'You get a handful of them and you can eat them or boil them to make tea. It is a trip like LSD but not so out of control. But a friend of ours just kept eating them and he cracked up. He still isn't the same. He sits for hours talking to himself. You can get sick and vomit or just have a pain in your stomach. But you feel like you're floating or looking down at yourself. You only get hallucinations if you eat lots and lots.' One of the major dangers is that poisonous mushrooms may be gathered and eaten. As with other hallucinogens the mental state of the user is the core issue and some individuals can move into short and long term psychosis.

Mescaline

Derived from the peyote cactus, this is dried and cut into slices. It is also refined into powder. It is commonly used in Ireland and the UK.

DMT

Derived from the seeds of South American plants.

PCP

This is phencyclidine and was manufactured as a veterinary anaesthetic. It is produced illegally and it is known as Angel Dust or the Peace Pill. It gives feelings of weightlessness, diminished body size and distortion of perception. It can result in a very frightening experience.

Overdosing results in vomiting, agitation, disorientation, respiratory problems and convulsions. It can cause prolonged coma.

Ketamine Hydrochloride

This is a white crystalline powder, usually known as 'K' or 'Special K'. It can also be obtained in tablet form. It is chemically related to PCP and is used for its hallucinogenic properties. However it is very dangerous. It is a short acting general anaesthetic. Recovery is slow and may be accompanied by nausea and vomiting. Headache, dizziness and confusion occurs. There may be nightmares, hallucinations, irrational and psychotic behaviour.

Often 'K' is sold as Ecstasy. It can cause numbness, blackouts, and temporary blindness.

GBH
This is another anaesthetic often sold as another drug, for example Ecstasy, with similar side effects and danger of convulsions and respiratory arrest. There are frightening examples of how young people can buy drugs and not know what they are buying and taking into their bodies.

Telltale signs of hallucinogens
• Blank vacant stares
• Inappropriate and extended interest in common objects
• Anxiety caused by no apparent reason
• Highly strung behaviour
• Loss of appetite
• Sweating
• Dilated pupils

6 Opiates/Narcotics
Within this category lie all those drugs which are derived from opium. They are extremely potent and highly addictive. Even under medical supervision patients can form a physical dependence. They may derive from the opium poppy or be produced synthetically. They include opium, morphine, heroin and codeine.

These are strong sleep-inducing painkillers, also known as analgesics. Opium contains morphine and codeine, both very effective painkillers. Heroin is easily manufactured from morphine in even the crudest laboratories. The medical profession uses opiates to relieve extreme pain from serious injury, or terminal illness such as cancer . As well as relieving pain opiates cause drowsiness. Heroin was devised as a safe substitute for morphine by a British chemist in 1874. It was marketed in 1898 as a cough suppressant. It was quickly realised that heroin was four times more addictive than morphine. Heroin is no longer available in Ireland for medical use. Codeine is used for less severe pain, often in combination with aspirin and paracetamol. Cough bottles with codeine have long been a widely abused product by young people, particularly those already into opiates. Extracts of opium are also included in various anti-diarrhoea preparations.

Many synthetic opiates are misused at street level. Pethidine, often used in childbirth, was widely abused in Ireland at one stage. Dipipanone is another painkiller sold under the name of Diconol, which has been abused here. Methadone, Physeptone linctus, is used to wean heroin addicts from heroin by blocking withdrawal symptoms. It is also used as part of programmes where addicts are maintained on a dose which keeps withdrawal symptoms at bay in order to minimise the risk to them and others by preventing the need to buy illegal drugs and the need to resort to crime. Unfortunately a lot of Physeptone comes on the black market and is abused by young addicts, both by those who are already using opiates and those who are starting to venture into this category and are afraid of other alternatives like morphine and heroin.

Two new synthetic opiates are dihydrocodeine DF118 and buprenorphine Temgesic, and both are frequently abused by young addicts. They buy them on the street from dealers who are young people themselves, and who are trying to make money to keep themselves in drugs.

Opiates can be swallowed, dissolved in water and injected. Heroin can be sniffed up the nose or smoked.

Many young addicts, when using opiates use the synthetic opiates especially Temgesic, Physeptone and Diconal. Morphine sulphate tablets known as Naaps or MSTs have become widely available and abused. These are additionally dangerous because the young addicts crush and inject them even though additives in their manufacture make injection more hazardous.

Opium

Opium is usually smoked. This is called 'chasing the dragon'. A small piece is placed in a roll of tinfoil and heated while the fumes are inhaled. Initially there is enhanced imagination and stimulation, which changes quickly into confused thinking, sleep and even coma.

Morphine

This is found in powder, tablet and liquid or ampoule form. Users take it by swallowing, drinking, injecting, inhaling and even as a suppository. Morphine powder is white. Napps come in various colours according to dosage and are all marked strength and Napp.

The euphoria produced by morphine can quickly develop into an overwhelming urge to continue using it. Sometimes an individual will suffer nausea, vomiting, constipation, confusion and sweating. This can be accompanied by fainting, palpitations, restlessness and mood changes, dry mouth and high facial colours. An overdose leads to respiratory arrest and even to coma or death. Withdrawal varies according to individual and their degree of dependence but has similar symptoms to heroin. Signs include, anxiety, yawning, sneezing, headache, weakness, restlessness, sweating, insomnia, nausea, vomiting, tremors and cramps.

KEITH

Keith has been depending on alcohol and other drugs for most of his teenage years now. Last summer he made a new contact, a guy called Charlie. Charlie is an old mate of Keith's cousin and the three of them spent a good deal of time together over those months. They had drugs in common. Charlie introduced Keith to Physeptone and DF118s. At first Keith felt wary because he believed that would be moving into dangerous waters. However one weekend, from dropping acid, Keith decided to give it a try. To his surprise he loved it. He reckoned after that that if he only used at weekends, he wouldn't have any problem. Charlie himself injected morphine sulphate or Naaps as he called them. He also carried DF118s as he sold them to get money for Naaps. After a while Keith tried the DF118s as well. It didn't seem to be too bad to be dropping a little white tablet, much as swallowing a liquid seemed OK. Keith convinced himself that though Charlie was obviously a junkie, he was only a weekend user, still in control. Over the following months Keith found himself regularly making the trek over the city to where Charlie hung out, on the pretence of visiting his cousin. He always knew where Charlie would be: either at a corner of the local shopping area where he and a group of drug users spent most of their afternoons or at the old house where he knew Charlie went to inject. Keith was a bit anxious about visiting these haunts at first but as time went on he grew bolder and more accustomed to the atmosphere. It was a horrible sight: young guys were sitting around stoned. Until they got to know Keith to see, he kept hovering nearby until he spied Charlie. Charlie supplied him with DF118s and eventually morphine sulphate tablets. Keith swallowed these, swearing to himself he would never inject. On a few occasions he smoked heroin, again telling himself it was a one-off situation and that as he was not injecting, it would be OK. Keith's mother was getting very concerned. She noticed how often recently he came in very restless, even hyper. His face would be red and his eyes staring. He would busy himself helping her, offering to make cups of tea and fussing around the kids. She knew something was wrong but kept denying it to herself.

Heroin
Heroin is the strongest analgesic known, five to eight times more powerful than morphine.

The purity of heroin bought on the street is an unknown quantity to the user. It may contain drugs such as phenobarbitone, paracetamol or caffeine. It is also cut or bulked to increase profit, with such substances as flour, lactose, talcum powder, glucose, powdered soup, curry powder or even plaster or brick dust. When injected, heroin produces a rapid 'rush' lasting less than a minute followed by a pleasant dreamlike state of peacefulness and contentment. It is a depressant so it slows the pulse, reduces the blood pressure, and relaxes the muscles.

Telltale signs
A person who is high on heroin will exhibit:
• Poor co-ordination
• Slowed reflexes
• Slurred speech
• Constricted pupils, glazed or watery eyes
• A face feverishly flushed

The first experience is often unpleasant with nausea and vomiting.

82

Heroin and other opiates mimic the effects of endomorphins, chemicals naturally occurring in the brain. Tolerance develops rapidly, which means that addicts take larger and larger amounts to get the same effect. Overdose is a primary risk and is more common among those who are just beginning to experiment or use it only occasionally. A single dose of heroin can cause deep unconsciousness and death. Dependence can occur after a few days. Withdrawal symptoms are called 'cold turkey' because of the chills and gooseflesh which are part of withdrawal. For some users, withdrawal may be like a mild flu. It depends on the extent of drug use. Symptoms are similar to withdrawal form morphine: yawning, tears, runny nose, sneezing, tremors, headache, sweating, anxiety, irritability, insomnia, spontaneous orgasm, loss of appetite, nausea, vomiting, diarrhoea, cramps and muscle spasms.

Most physical damage is due to using dirty needles or sharing needles. Blood-poisoning can occur. Adulterants which do not dissolve cause abcesses, clots in the lungs, gangrene and loss of limbs. A severe viral hepatitis can be got from sharing a needle. It can also cause liver cancer. AIDS has become the most ominous risk of needle-sharing.

The side-effects of opiates, including heroin, include reduced sex drive, constipation, palpitations, rashes and itching especially of the nose. Disturbed sleeping habits may develop. As tolerance builds, anger and depression increasingly accompany the high, as the euphoric effects grow milder and milder. Most of the euphoria seems to occur at the earlier stages of use, and those who are truly addicted experience little euphoria. Personal hygiene suffers. Dietary needs are ignored. Constipation will be chronic. Sexual relations are virtually non-existent as chronic heavy opiate use impairs sexual functioning and reduces interest in sex.

PATRICK

Patrick mainlines heroin. He always loved coke and tried speedballs, a mixture of cocaine and heroin. For Patrick it was an obvious move to start smoking and skinpopping heroin. This was where he would inject heroin just below the skin. He tried snorting heroin as well. From the beginning he fell in love with the drug and moved very quickly into using it almost exclusively. He was moving more and more away from his old friends, though he still hung around in order to sell drugs to pay for his heroin. He bought quarters (packs of four doses) almost from the beginning, telling himself it was cheaper that way but found himself using it all much quicker than he had anticipated. Sometimes he would get the heroin in town in a pub, in the corner of a plastic bag. It would have been in someone's mouth and he'd have to put it in his own so that it could be easily hidden if he was stopped. Patrick was prepared to swallow it if necessary. He very quickly found that if he hadn't any heroin he became restless and uneasy. As he began to feel weak and trembly and his eyes became watery, Patrick would know he had to have heroin. He could keep the withdrawals away with methadone tablets, Physeptone or codeine. Sometimes he would take a good few drinks and some sleeping tablets like Dalmaine or Rohypnol and that helped. Once he began to mainline, to inject directly into his veins, or his arms and hands, Patrick knew he would keep on injecting, though he didn't like to admit it. He liked it much more than smoking. He also discovered Temgesic and he would inject them but they became impossible to get. He also used Palfium tablets. Patrick's whole life now was revolving around getting heroin, or a nearly acceptable substitute.

Paraphernalia of heroin use: spoons, matches, tinfoil, drinking straws, small folder pieces of paper (from street deals—wraps), paper hankies.

Methadone
Available in several forms: white powder, tablets, injection ampoules and linctus. The linctus is either brown or green, depending on strength.

Side effects are lightheadedness, dizziness, nausea, sweating. It too can lead to respiratory arrest, coma and death.

Tell-tale signs of opiate abuse
- Small pupils/dilated pupils
- Needle marks
- Raw red nostrils
- Nausea, vomiting
- Restlessness, distraction
- Incoherence

- Flushed face
- Lethargy, drowsy behaviour at inappropriate times
- Euphoria
- Constant need for money
- Detachment from reality

Young people experiment in all categories of drugs. Some stay with their preferred drug, for example alcohol and cannabis or ecstasy and acid. Often they believe that if they don't inject they are not 'junkies'. Unfortunately the more they experiment, the more they use. The more they use, the more they need to use to get the same effect. The more and more they use, the more drugs become normalised. Where once alcohol and hash was a big deal, acid, speed and ecstasy now just seem like the normal, average thing to do. Because they are choosing to drug, they mix with other people who are using their preferred drug in the place where the drug is available.

It often appears to young people as if their drug taking is the obvious, even the only thing to do. They do not believe they could be addicted, and see their drug use as social or occasional. Often as they move further into experimentation they get braver (or more desensitised) and end up trying drugs they would have originally shunned, cocaine, morphine derivatives, sleeping tablets, tranquillisers and heroin. Once they are using drugs they will often substitute one for another, and eventually as their tolerance increases, start to use them together to get a greater or longer 'buzz'.

Often young people take drugs not knowing what they are putting into their body or the consequences for their short-term and long-term health. Not only are they unaware of the effects of the drugs, but often they are sold other drugs instead. They take tablets which could be anything and mix them either inadvertently with other drugs which could be lethal, or indiscriminately, not even thinking about how they will react, not caring what they are taking. As we have seen, many drugs are adulterated with toxic substances or other drugs. Also dealers push drugs which are really a different substance, for example amphetamines as Ecstasy, or anaesthetics such as Letamine sold as Ecstasy, or PCP sold as LSD. This ignorance and risk-taking increases the dangers of drugs, as does mixing.

Chapter Six

What is Addiction?

Most people have an answer to this question, their own description of an addict, usually based on their personal experience. However, much of the time, there is confusion about the nature of addiction, its basis and origin and the type of people who become addicted. This confusion can lead to individuals avoiding and/or denying the existence of addiction in themselves or in someone close to them. They may think someone is too young or too nice or too sensible to become addicted. People often have their own prejudices about addicts based on the behavioural and psychological consequences of abusing drugs which they have seen or heard about, for example stealing, lying, neglect of hygiene and violence.

A drug can be defined as a chemical which causes changes in the way the human body functions, mentally, physically or emotionally. Any person who misuses a drug for a long period of time is at risk of dependency. There are two separate components to dependency, often confused: physical dependency and psychological dependency. Physical dependency may result from a body's adapting to repeated use of a drug and if the drug is stopped there may be a reaction in the body similar to physical symptoms of illness. This in itself is not addiction. People using tranquillisers under medical supervision may develop a physical dependency—their body has got used to the drug's presence and reacts to its absence—and yet not be 'addicted'.

Repeated drug use can cause a body to adapt in other ways. For example, the drug may be eliminated or metabolised more quickly, which means its effect is lost more quickly; or the cells of the brain may adapt and more of the drug be required to give the same effect. This is known as tolerance.

Physical dependency is relatively easy to treat. This is done either by giving the body time to return to its normal functioning or by giving carefully monitored doses of another drug which block the withdrawal symptoms and which are gradually decreased. For example, methadone is used to help heroin addicts to withdraw.

Not all drugs cause physical dependency. Avoidance of withdrawal symptoms can play a role in the development of addiction, as can psychological factors through the reinforcing nature of many drugs, that is the reward in terms of pleasure, feelings of well-being, calm or excitement. Many drugs are believed to work by replicating the effects of naturally produced painkillers in the brain or by fitting into receptor sites in the cells of the body, like a key in a lock, giving pleasurable messages to the body.

In simple terms, someone who is addicted is someone who has a personal relationship with a drug or drugs which has become 'sick'. Any of our relationships can become unhealthy. We can become sick in our relation to other people, in our love affairs. We can have sick relationships with power, sex, food, gambling, other drugs. Anything that is desirable to us can become the focus of our attention. It can start to preoccupy us, then obsess us. It can then begin to interfere with our functioning in and relating to other aspects of our life and becomes the centre of our attention and energy to the detriment of other areas; it has become sick or unhealthy.

Addiction is essentially, 'a sick or pathological relationship of a person to a mood-altering chemical substance in expectation of a rewarding experience' (McAuliffe and McAuliffe).

Because all normal human beings to feel better and to perceive and act differently at times, we are all candidates for a relationship with a drug. The misuse of drugs occurs when there is a potential for harm in that relationship. The abuse of drugs occurs when it brings actual harm or injury. Sometimes the harm may be relatively slight. Harm does not mean disaster and unfortunately the abuse of alcohol and other drugs is often recognised only when the results are approaching disaster. The line between abuse and dependency is very fine, if it exists at all.

Consider getting drunk or stoned, losing control of yur judgement, concentration, body reflexes, muscles, emotions and even losing consciousness. This is obviously abuse. It can happen to anyone. However, people do not usually repeat harmful and dangerous experiences. Drug abuse repeated to the point of danger is a sign of drug dependency.

Drug abuse is both a precursor and a symptom of drug addiction. It may then be defined as the use of any drug, legal or illegal, which damages some aspect of the users' life, whether it is their mental or physical health, their relationship with their family, friends or with their work or hobbies. This definition includes not only the use of illegal drugs but also the dangerous use of legal drugs such as alcohol and tobacco, the harmful use of prescribed medicines by exceeding the prescribed dose, and the illegal use of legal drugs, for example in underage drinking, driving and so on. The fact that a drug is legal and socially acceptable does not mean that it causes less harm or damage. Indeed the more the use of a drug becomes socially acceptable, the greater the capacity for harm. Alcohol, for example, is the drug most often implicated in violence, murder, road accidents and accidental death.

Often, when we worry about drugs, we may think of addiction as the main hazard for users. Many young people abuse drugs but do not become addicted. This is not to say there is no need for worry or concern. The abuse of a drug has many physical and psychological dangers and these exist even if a young person abuses for a relatively short period of time or may affect even at first use. Obviously many of the risks increase as abuse continues over a period of time. Indeed the risk of addiction increases as abuse is repeated but there are risks related to factors other than time. When we are talking to or about young people and drugs, it is essential to make clear not only the dangers of addiction but also the dangers of abuse. Often the confusion about whether or not a young person is addicted or 'how to know when there is addiction and when not', can mask the importance of minimising the risks involved when young people use drugs. Because of the 'nature of the beast' it can be difficult, even impossible, to protect a young person totally from a relationship with drugs. Because of curiosity, the need to act independently—even rebelliously, to fit in with peers, to belong and because of the desire to explore and experience new sensations and situations and because we live in a drug culture, young people will usually experiment. They need to know about the dangers of drug abuse also.

Many of the problems caused by drugs are related to increased dosage. This is very important. When South Americans chewed the cocoa plant the small amounts of cocaine taken were not particularly harmful. However smoking highly concentrated crack can result in death or rapid development of addiction. Many dangerous situations are caused by young people initially experimenting with a drug and taking too much. This can result in fatal overdose. Young people are also inclined to bravado , taking more and more of a drug in order to impress their friends, like Frank and his friends daring one another as to who could take most Ecstasy tablets. Often drugs are regarded as harmless but it is only when they become more popular and are used more often and at higher doses, that the harmful effects can be seen.

Drugs can be taken in many different ways. The speed and intensity of the high, as well as its duration, are often related to the way the drug is taken. The amount of drugs absorbed and distributed in the body depends on the method of ingestion: for example, cocaine when smoked is faster, more potent and capable of being absorbed for much longer than when snorted. The intensity of the effect is controlled by the rate at which it is eliminated, for example, the greater 'rush' is when heroin is injected rather than smoked. The more intense the 'rush' or 'buzz', the greater the chance of developing dependency. Intravenous injection, smoking and sniffing cause more rapid onset of drug action than chewing, eating or injections under the skin. Injection carries the greatest risk of fatal overdose because higher concentrations of the drug can be achieved and because injecting needs proper skill. Lack of hygiene in preparation and injecting and the sharing of needles leads to the spread of disease, for example, hepatitis B and AIDS. In September 1993, 159 of 362 cases of AIDS reported in Ireland were intravenous drug users; 52 per cent of HIV positive individuals are intravenous drug users and one study reported that 63 per cent continued to share injecting equipment after being diagnosed as being HIV positive.

A person's weight can affect how much of the drug is absorbed. Lighter individuals get greater effects and are thus in great danger from a similar quantity of drug. Gender plays a role. A girl will react differently from her male counterpart because of the different water and fat content of her body. The less body fat the higher the concentration of the drug in the blood. When food has been consumed, particularly fatty food, the absorption of alcohol into the blood can be slowed down.

If two or more drugs are taken together the effects are difficult to gauge. When drugs are combined, there may be dangerous consequences, as the combined effects may be greater than the sum of their individual effects. Alcohol is the drug most often combined. Fatal overdoses occur more easily when tranquillisers, for instance, are used with alcohol. Alcohol and cannabis make another prevalent combination. Cannabis increases the sedative effects of alcohol with increased risk of accidents. Since drugs remain in the body for varying periods, often hours or even days, the two substances don't even have to be taken at the same time.

If you buy your drugs on the 'street' (black market) then you have no guarantee that the drug you have bought is what it is supposed to be, nor do you know of what purity the drug is. Often drugs are contaminated through backstreet manufacture or intentionally to bulk them up to increase profits. These added agents may be dangerous or may cause ulceration and clogging when injected.

An individual's personality, emotional maturity and stability have great bearing on how a drug will affect them. An average hallucinatory trip say on LSD could push an already emotionally vulnerable or mentally unstable young person over the edge, sometimes irretrievably.

Your surroundings influense how the drug effects you, for example whether it is a rave or a quiet place. Your mood and state of mind play an often crucial role . When you are down or depressed you could drink a lot of alcohol in search of a high but never achieve it. This is the 'I couldn't get drunk' syndrome. However, the alcohol will still affect your body and mind, though the high is not achieved.

These are all aspects of drug use of which young people should be aware in order to increase the hopes of their making informed and responsible choices even within the framework of experimentation, if that is what they are determined on. So though young people often cannot be totally restrained from using drugs, they may learn to minimise the risks to their minds and bodies.

The problems caused by drug taking:

1 Damage can be caused by the way a drug acts on the body. We have already explored this in the section on brain and liver damage caused by alcohol. Many drugs can lead to depression, or initiate or trigger pre-existing mental illness. For example, cannabis can trigger schizophrenia.

2 Damage can be caused by the way a drug is taken: septicaemia, hepatitis B, gangrene, AIDS can all be caused by injecting drugs.

3 Disinhibition caused by substances such as alcohol and cannabis can lead to unwanted pregnancy. When drug use is continued in pregnancy, the foetus is exposed to the drugs the mother is using. Instances of abnormalities of the heart, kidneys and bowel increase where mothers use cocaine during pregnancy, Mental retardation can be caused by the consumption of alcohol during pregnancy. There is a greater risk of miscarriage and stillbirth and sometimes a baby may be born drug-dependent. There is no evidence of any safe limit of drug use during pregnancy, so the advice must be not to take any drug, including alcohol, tobacco and caffeine while pregnant.

4 Effects on behaviour can be dangerous; people may take to climbing electric pylons while on acid or Ecstasy. Many drugs release aggressive tendencies by reducing inhibition. Other drugs alter our perception of the world and we may not react to pain, hunger or fatigue as we normally would. This means we may not safeguard or protect ourselves. For instance, dancing on a broken leg has been known.

5 Lifestyles can cause problems: living rough, self-neglect and overdosage.

6 Family relationships are damaged, neglected and often break-up occurs.

7 Crime is often associated with drugtaking. Many young addicts will steal to obtain money for drugs and will also deal illegal drugs. The high cost of drugs such as heroin means that users sometimes resort to prostitution, burglary or shoplifting. Heroin users do not tend to commit violent crimes but drugs like PCP or Angel Dust can cause violent responses. Paranoia resulting from cocaine and amphetamine use can lead to aggression. The drug most

implicated in violent crime is alcohol.

8 Most drugs damage coordination, reaction time and attention. This means that driving, using machinery, even crossing the road, all become more dangerous. In some studies the percentage of cannabis users killed and injured in road traffic accidents comes out the same as that for those drinking alcohol. These effects can be slow to wear off; cannabis still causes these effects three to four hours after the high has worn off.

9 An important consequence of drug use for young people is the harm done to intellectual performance, memory and learning ability. The damage to their education can affect their ability to gain employment. Their inability to gain skills and perform a job efficiently can lose them an apprenticeship or job.

Despite all these dangers and warnings of dangers, young people, some young people, will continue to use drugs. The more often they abuse drugs, any drug or any combination of drugs, the more likely it is that they will become drug-dependent, or addicted. The answer to whether someone is addicted or not lies in the nature of their relationship with drugs. When there is a deep personal commitment to their drugs, when they are choosing drugs over their family, friends, school, work, hobbies, girlfriends, when drugs have become their priority, their focus, their reason for living and everything else becomes secondary, then the young person can be said to have developed a 'love' relationship with drugs. This is addiction.

Chapter Seven

The Progress of Addiction

Drugs are powerful mood-changers, and it is this expected mood change that is the prime motivation for taking drugs. This desire to change their mood and to mask, change or escape their feelings, is at the core of addicts' relationship with drugs. How much they take, how often they take drugs and what they use are simply the symptoms of this primary 'love' relationship with drugs. This is true for all addictions to all forms of drugs.

Addicts are people who have become dependent on a mood-altering chemical. It becomes the focus of their thinking, their planning, their choices. All other relationships become secondary to the drug. Often the addiction is well progressed before others start to notice the changes or to grasp the meaning of the changes but the relationship with drugs is usually well established and is marked by the young person's commitment to drugs. Some young people have a preferred drug of use for example alcohol, morphine or heroin, and they will discount their use of other drugs. But it is the overall picture of drug use that must be explored, not just the use of illegal drugs or 'hard' drugs. Also the symptoms, or the damage, may seem relatively mild but the dependency may already be established.

Addiction is a complex and often confusing illness. Even after it became known, for example, that chronic use of opiates produces physical dependence, people continued to believe that to develop a dependence or to use opiates again after detoxification indicated a flawed, immoral character, and even low intelligence. This is something that most people who are not themselves in the grip of a chemical substance dependency find difficult, if not impossible, to understand. How can someone, knowing that they are putting their lives in danger, hurting those who love them and destroying their goals and dreams, continue to take a drug ?

Nowadays this is understood as the symptoms of a disease, a disease with recognisable symptoms and a predictable progression. Often the concept of addiction as a disease seems confusing because of the amount of conscious control a person has over beginning and ending drug use. Most diseases begin without our being aware of them and are not of our making. In contrast, drug addiction would seem to begin only if a person chooses and continues to choose to take drugs. But no one chooses to become addicted. The drug-taking may be self-inflicted but the addiction is not. This is one of the major problems and issues in the sphere of recovery from addiction. Often young people will want to stop the problems caused, halt the changes in themselves, live a more meaningful life but still hang on to the drug-taking. Most alcoholics go through the phase of wanting to be a social drinker and resent hugely the reality that they are not, cannot, and never will be social drinkers, no matter how many other people out there can be.

Addiction is not chosen: rather it is the destruction of an individual's free choice and the replacement of it with the conditions set down by their need to have drugs. Slowly but surely the people they spend time with, the places they go, what they do with their energy, time, money, how they spend their day, whether they eat or sleep—all these choices are determined by whether or not they will facilitate their drug use.

Tied up with these choices are changes in the personality of young people. They become more moody, more secretive, dishonest, more negative towards themselves and others, more preoccupied, selfish, uncaring, insensitive and even abusive. Because of disinhibition when using, there may be episodes of unruliness and aggressive, violent or unpredictable behaviour. They feel increasingly bad about themselves behind it all, and while this behaviour may be seen as who or what they are, it is primarily a symptom of their addiction. They are no longer Chris, Patrick, Tessa or Keith; they have become less themselves and more, if not all, an addiction.

CHRIS

Chris, as we have already seen, is an attractive and popular young man. From an outsider's point of view Chris had everything going for him. Certainly many of the other youngsters of his own age envied him. Chris comes from a home where his father drinks a lot of alcohol. To Chris his Dad is an alcoholic but no one else has ever used that term. His dad comes home, has his dinner, then goes to the pub again until bedtime. On Saturdays he sleeps late, has his dinner, which is at 12.30 p.m. sharp on Saturday then it's off to the pub for the rest of the day, watching the races on the TV and making a few bets, sending out for chips for his tea and coming home legless at bedtime. Sunday is much the same except he goes to the pub after church, comes home for his dinner at 1.00 p.m. sharp, sleeps for the afternoon and then goes back to the pub in the evening.

Chris's mother spoils him rotten. He is her baby and his two elder brothers slag him unmercifully about being the favourite. Nothing is ever asked of Chris: his meals are ready; his bed is made; his clothes are cleaned and ironed. Chris, however, was never as sure of himself as others thought. He worried a lot about his mother and always felt that his dad thought him a failure, a cissy, not the sort of son he wanted. Chris thought his dad disliked him and desperately tried to please him. This was difficult because his dad was rarely there. If he was, he was in a hurry out or drunk. At school Chris didn't concentrate very well. He often worried about his mum, who seemed to be constantly sad and tired. Because Chris was articulate, polite and even charming it was not obvious to others how much he was struggling to keep up in school. He worried about this and copied a lot from his pals. The girls in his class didn't seem to care anyway and eagerly gave him their work before school. Chris didn't let on that he couldn't remember or understand a lot that was going on.

When Chris was fourteen he discovered alcohol. From the very first time he loved it. He loved everything about it. He first drank just because he was curious, because it was the thing to do, because everyone else was doing it. He found it helped him to overcome his shyness, that it made it easier to belong with the lads, all together having a laugh, and he forgot to worry about his mum. He felt that at last he was grown up. It seemed to boost his self-confidence and it helped him to forget rows at home between his parents. He drank whenever he got the money. He'd drink in the park, in the fields, in the churchyard, in someone's home. From the beginning every penny he got went on cans. Then he tried hash. He loved that too. So he started to use alcohol and hash, sometimes both together but mostly smoking hash for several weeks, then swinging back to alcohol, then a few weeks later, back to hash again. His schoolwork went even further downhill and he started to skip days at school to hang about and smoke dope and play pool. His football fell by the wayside also because he hadn't time to go to matches or to practices.

As Chris was tall for his age; before long he was being served in pubs and his life became very like his dad's. Soon he was using other drugs, particularly speed (amphetamines), coke (cocaine) and Acid (LSD). He tried magic mushrooms (psilocybin) once or twice but had frightening trips and never bothered again. Once he smoked heroin and liked it so much that he tried to keep away from it. There seemed to be no problem in getting drugs. At the pub there were always joints and tablets being offered and he knew who to contact if he wanted some gear (drugs). He would drink any kind of alcoholic drink he could lay his hands on. To wake in a corner somewhere at two or three or four in the morning became second nature to him. He knew his mum was worried and would be awake waiting for him to come in. She'd ask him where he'd been but he'd spin her some yarn and she couldn't question it. He knew he was shutting her up, because if she pushed it at all he'd get narky and cross and start giving out about something else. He knew she was not able to challenge him; she was so afraid of a row she'd do anything to keep the peace. She never said anything to his dad either and at night his dad would be conked out from his own booze.

Chris constantly lied about where he'd been, who he'd been with, what he was doing. He'd get money for school books he didn't need, or charities that didn't exist. He'd get money for lunches at school that was spent on drink and drugs. He'd steal from his brothers, his dad and his mother's purse. He guessed his dad would never know how much he had left when he came home from the pub, but he figured his mother would realise that money was missing. Sometimes he stole things from home to sell.

Chris had a long line of girlfriends. He never allowed any

of them to get close but he would try them out for sex. He loved sex when he was using but he never wanted to let any of the girls matter. He was popular but he didn't really care about anyone. That was until Anna came on the scene. He thought he liked her but he still found himself lying to her about being late for dates, about lack of money, about how much he had to drink before he met her. He'd always say one or two pints though it was usually five or six pints—and a couple of joints. He always drank and smoked before a date because Anna was too slow for him and though they had only been going out for a while she was already saying things like, 'Have you not had enough?' ; 'I'd like to go now'; 'How many pints do you drink in a night?'.

He had wondered at Anna's getting involved with him because he knew he had a bad reputation, not only for dropping girls but also for getting into fights. He knew he got very violent when he took speed. Without warning he would start picking fights with anyone at all and then start throwing punches. His greatest shame was the fact that he had hit a previous girlfriend and he hoped no one would ever know that. His mood would swing around over nothing; he'd feel irritable and angry or else be sullen and withdrawn. If he was broke he'd go home, talk to no one and lock himself in his room. Once he had lost his temper with his mum and grabbed a lamp and smashed it against the wall. Mostly when he got home he was drunk. The next day he would apologise to his mum, tell her it would never happen again and try his best to be nice to her.

After the lamp episode he felt embarrassed and ashamed but told himself it was the drink and drugs that was the cause and that he hadn't meant it. He did his best to forget it and eventually he pushed that to the back of his mind along with all the other worrying episodes: like the time he had broken the back door window to get in when he had lost his key, and cut his hand badly. He was so high he didn't even notice and went straight to bed. He might have bled badly, even if not to death, except that his mum had heard the noise. Or the time he had crashed his motorbike with a passenger on the pillion. He had been tripping (drugging) all day and had fallen asleep while driving. Or the times he got sick in the sink or fell asleep on the loo, waking up cold and stiff hours later. Once he had intended to have a quick bath and his dad had to break down the door. He had got very angry with them on that occasion when they accused him of using drugs, saying he had just fallen asleep. He knew he could have drowned but felt his dad had a cheek when it was only what he himself had been doing all Chris's life.

Chris had become very adept at putting these kind of memories behind him; so that he didn't remember them unless reminded of them. He also stopped giving much thought to anyone's feelings, cares or worries. He never stopped to think if he was hurting anyone; just did what he pleased. However he could be charming when he wanted, if it meant getting his own way. Very gradually Chris was being destroyed by chemicals—his sense of self, his goals, his values, his standards, his morals, his relationships were all at risk. Even when he knew something was wrong with his attitude to drink and drugs, he continued to use, pretending even to himself that he was enjoying himself. He had become completely dishonest. His stealing had now progressed to breaking into cars to rob stereos, even grabbing money from people who were using PIN machines. On a couple of occasions he had broken into houses, just looking for something to sell to buy drugs. He was an expert shoplifter, taking something nearly every day. There was a particular street in another area where he always knew he had a market, chatting up the old girls and promising them something special the next time! The only time he really spoke to his mum was when he thought he stood a chance of borrowing (or begging) a few quid. He knew he would never pay her back. When he was with the family he was rude and uncooperative, making snide comments, complaining and just waiting for opportunity to get away. Chris never ate with the family any more; in fact he rarely ate at all. His weight has dropped and he is frighteningly thin, though tall. He is only 9st 2lb, though he is nearly six foot. He is constantly sick, catching one virus after another. Even though he has a weak chest and is always getting chest infections, he continues to smoke cigarettes and hash, not caring what they are doing to his lungs.

He has lost all interest in his schoolwork, not caring about his results, hardly attending school never mind studying.

Even when he tries to concentrate on books in which he is interested, he finds it extremely difficult. He can't remember specific details of anything, even films or TV programmes

Chris just doesn't care any more. He wants to care about Anna, but doesn't know how to go about that; to feel anything other than apathy or anger is very scary. His feelings for her keep highlighting the fact that his drugs are getting in the way of his life. He promises himself that he won't use or he'll use less when he's with Anna but he keeps messing up. He still takes a few pints or some hash or some speed. He keeps telling himself he doesn't care; all he needs is a few more pints or a few joints and that everything is OK. But deep inside, he knows he is lying to himself. He is still dealing drugs, ever since Patrick offered him a bag of 100 acid tabs and anything else he could shift at a reasonable price. He knows if he messes this up, he could end up seriously damaged. Everyone has heard horror stories of guys needing umpteen stitches, having broken limbs, smashed faces and other damage after not paying their bills. Chris buys his personal drugs in bulk, always paying cash, so that the dealer will always get in touch with him when he has new stuff. He lends people money so that when they pay him back he'll have money for drink. Money just goes straight out his pocket, always on drink and drugs. He hides bottles of drink everywhere at home, in the toilet cistern, in the attic, under the stairs, in his pockets, under the mattress; he even sews the sleeves of coats to hide bottles in. He hides drugs in hollowed-out books on his bookshelf, in the shed, in his mother's plants, stuck under chairs—anywhere he thinks they are safe.

All his friends are also drug users. His mother keeps blaming them, saying they are a bad influence. But Chris sticks with them because he knows that he fits in, that they won't question his behaviour no matter how bizarre. When he doesn't remember arrangements made in the pub, they don't even seem to notice. Often Chris doesn't remember anything he said, and has only the vaguest recollections of arguments and fights which he has usually caused. His mates seem to see this as normal. Chris is still only eighteen years old, and unless he is helped to recognise that his relationship with alcohol and drugs will gradually ruin his lifestyle, his relationships and eventually his very life, he is already truly lost to himself and others.

Chris's story is the classic example of how young people can initially experiment with drugs with all the usual motivation, and become enmeshed in addiction. Frighteningly they can be involved to this degree without their family or teachers properly realising it . Often they know something is wrong, may even suspect it and yet be totally unaware of the full picture.

Initially Chris took drugs out of curiosity. He liked the effect and he began to use drugs for the pleasure they gave and the mood change involved. Before long he was medicating all his uncomfortable feelings, anxiety, disappointment, anger, fear, sadness, with drugs, as well as using them in a social setting. Drugging, that is using alcohol, cannabis, speed and acid, is now his method of dealing with stress as well as a way of finding pleasure. This is the initial stage of dependency. He began to need more and more drugs to get the same effect and seemed to be able eventually to take a lot of drugs without any apparent ill-effect. He had blackouts and episodes of aggressive or unreasonable behaviour. He hid his inner worries by drugging more. Chris has now moved into another stage of dependency. In time, despite all the justifications he invents for himself, Chris has reached the stage where he no longer has the ability to decide whether he will drug or not, nor the ability to know for sure how much he will use when he does drug. He no longer can guarantee what state he will end up in. This is a further stage of dependency, that of 'loss of control'. His powerlessness over his use of drugs is symptomised by the lengths to which he is now prepared to got to get his alcohol and drugs.

As Chris continues to break the promises he has made to himself, to act in a way that is embarrassing, shameful and frightening and as he begins to do things which are basically against his principles, values and morals in order to get a supply of drugs, his self-esteem gets lower and lower and his self-hatred increases. The conflict caused by this and also that stirred up by people about whom Chris cares but whom he is disappointing and hurting and those who threaten his drug supply or use of drugs in any way, is extremely threatening. So threatening that it feels life-threatening to Chris, who by now believes that unless he has drugs he will not be able to do anything, not even talk to anyone—he will not be able to cope with life.

He is now living to drug. The thought of a day without drugs is physically, emotionally and mentally unbearable. Chris has many physical symptoms related to his drug abuse. He is inefficient, fatigued. He finds it difficult to sleep, has little appetite and is susceptible to infection. He is increasingly moody and difficult, feeling quite paranoid and suspicious of people, cynical and negative in his attitude towards everything. He often experiences tremors in his hands and a sense of dread and foreboding. Unless someone intervenes in his drugging or a crisis occurs which forces him to look at his life and what is happening because of his relationship with drugs, he will move only further into self-destruction.

His attempts to deal with the conflict caused by his drugging have only resulted in the development of delusion, where the dependent person does not see the reality of how he is living nor is in touch with the emotional consequences. Chris knows his mother is worried but he does not really know or empathise with her constant state of anxiety, preoccupation and fear for his safety. She is living on her nerves, full of frustration, hurt and anger about the way he is behaving. She does not know how to help him and does not want to antagonise or reject him in case it makes matters worse.

The first thing Chris thinks about in the morning is drugs. He always keeps some cannabis near him, already rolled in a joint, so that he can smoke some before he does anything else. His obsession with the drug is total. All his physical and mental energy goes into maintaining his relationship, his supply. However this is largely subconscious and hidden from his awareness. His defences protect him from the conflict and threat of this reality and he believes that he is quite aware of his involvement with drugs. Because of this preoccupation Chris is not available to others. He cannot give full attention to them; he is not able to concentrate; nor is he prepared to be honest with them. He is not capable of relating properly to others. Emotionally he has detached himself. He has taught himself or chosen not to care about himself or others, because it is too threatening to his drugs and therefore too painful. He denies the reality of his situation in many ways. He minimises

101

the amount he is using and lies constantly to everyone about the quantities involved. Not even Patrick nor his dealer knows how much Chris takes. He lies to everyone, even about inconsequential issues, and so confuses issues all the time. He has all sorts of justifications and reasons to explain away his drug taking: Everyone uses drugs nowadays, I'm in control, I'm not injecting...When his drugging causes problems he blames everyone around, his mates, his girlfriends, rather than question his own behaviour. As he dislikes himself more and more he withdraws further and further from others.

Chris, like other young addicts, is not a morally bad person but a critically ill human being. He has a secret life which he attempts to hide behind the smiling charm he presents to those who know him only casually. Those who are more involved wonder at the Jekyll and Hyde character. They are watching Chris slowly kill himself, his spirit first and then his body.

Chapter Eight

The Effect on the family:
Enabling and Intervention

TESSA

When the gardai arrived at Tessa's home, her father's first reaction was one of disbelief. 'Not my Tessa!' he exclaimed. All through that first evening, while he, his wife, Tessa and Fred sat in the front room, George continued to refuse to believe what he was hearing. He took Tessa's part, wanting to believe all the justifications Tessa was giving, putting his arms around the sobbing girl and comforting her. He was angry with the gardai for believing that his Tessa, his little girl would steal or plan to steal. Margaret, on the other hand, had to be restrained by one of the gardai from screaming at Tessa. She was beside herself with anger. 'The shame of it, in front of all the neighbours, bringing the law to our front door, you little hussy. You never think of anyone but yourself. In and out like a bloody hotel, where's this, where's that, I want this, I want that.' The next minute Margaret was sobbing uncontrollably. She could hardly hear what the gardai were saying but the odd phrase go through: 'feel it's not the first time'; 'want to make an example'; 'intend to press charges'; 'I'm afraid you'll have to come to the station.'

When George and Tessa had gone, Margaret sat in her front room and looked at Fred. He had remained silent throughout the whole episode, amidst all the anger and recriminations. 'Do you think she did it, son?' Margaret asked him. 'You know she did it , mum. You know she took my walkman and your gold chain and that she's been taking money out of your purse and our pockets for months. Why wouldn't she take something from someone else?' 'I know, I know. It'll break your dad's heart. He won't believe it. She can never put a foot wrong as far as he's concerned.'

Fred sighed. 'Mum, it's more than just stealing. I know it is. You both need to listen to me. I'm not imagining things or making them up. I think, I *know* she's on drugs. Where do you think she goes every weekend. Do you really believe she's at Sandra's, Joan's or Betty's ? She's so rude, so out of it, you know she's changed over the last year.' Fred stopped because his mother was crying even more loudly. He felt sick to the stomach but relieved somewhere inside himself. Perhaps now he could offload some of this sense of responsibility, this burden he had been carrying since he first put two and two together all those months before. He had tackled Tessa himself times without number and had been met with hostility, threats and even hatred. When he approached her in anger, about something she had done or her total lack of care and concern, she had reacted with denial, lies and abuse. When he approached her in care and worry, she had shrugged and laughed off his concern saying: 'You're just a prude. Why don't you go out and have a good time? You just can't take it that I'm like other people, that I know how to enjoy myself and you just want to be a holy Joe.' At times he wondered if he was imagining things, or if he was exaggerating and getting things out of proportion, or even if he really was jealous. He wondered if he was the one who was getting things wrong. Mostly he was up and down, very angry with her or very guilty that he couldn't get his parents to see what he could see. They were good people but they were caught up in their own life, their ballroom dancing, their group of friends, he and his dogs, she and the housework. He could see that his mum got annoyed with Tessa and there were constant battles between the two of them about what Tessa wasn't doing or what she was wearing or why she wasn't eating or what time she was coming home. But they never seemed to see the wood for the trees. He hoped that this time there would be some straight talking, that they would talk about what was happening for Tessa instead of just roaring at her as his mum usually did, or avoiding the issue as his dad usually did. He didn't know what they could do but somehow he felt that if they just talked about it, maybe Tessa would admit the truth.

When a family is dealing with a drug problem, often it is within their midst for a long time before they either see it or know about it. Even when the signs are very obvious, and there is no way of avoiding the effects of the drugtaking, family members react in ways that best help them as individuals, and the family as a whole copes and survive. Sometimes these methods of coping are ones which do not help the young person involved and which are harmful to the family members themselves. They often look back in astonishment at the way they enabled the drug-taking to continue. However their behaviour is their genuine best effort to preserve the normal functioning of the home and they are always acting in the best interests (as they see it) of everyone involved.

Knowing that your son or daughter, brother or sister or even friend is on drugs can be devastating. You may find out by accident by stumbling upon something which makes you ask questions or you may hear something from a friend or from one of your other children. Or you may hear for the first time when the school or workplace contacts you, or the gardai come to your door. Sometimes families and friends learn about a young person's drug relationship not in any dramatic way, but through a number of small factors which add up to an uncomfortable, sad and frightening picture. They may notice extreme dips and swings in mood, patterns of eating and sleeping, a change from openness, honesty and communication to secretiveness, sullenness even aggression, that, even allowing for the troubled times of adolescence, seem to be outside the normal. They may, to their horror, notice that money is going missing or that beloved possessions are disappearing.

KEITH

Keith's mother's heart sank when his beloved guitar disappeared. She knew the situation had been disimproving despite all her best efforts to be supportive to him. She had believed that it was a bad patch he was going through, that he had too many responsibilities for a young man and that he deserved to kick up his heels and rebel in some way. He was a good, quiet and loyal son, and she had attempted to be loyal to him in her own way by pretending that she didn't notice the way he was withdrawing and opting out of the family. More and more he was staying out late and not giving her as much money (though he still gave her some). He hardly spoke to her any more except to mumble at her as he went upstairs.

The younger kids were heartbroken, particularly Ben, who

was next to Keith in age and idolised him. There was five years between Ben and Keith, but Ben wanted to go everywhere with Keith. The mother knew Keith was too old to have a little brother in tow but she wished he would give him some time every now and then. Keith had always taken such interest in Ben and his football; it nearly made up for their lack of a dad. Now he didn't bother with Ben or the little ones, often eating their heads off for the slightest thing. This wasn't the Keith she knew, who was gentle and kind. She prayed every night that he would be all right and that he wouldn't get hooked on drink or on anything else. She noticed the face on him when he came home sometimes. It was in his eyes. They'd look red and watery a lot of the time and he moved so slowly and spoke so strangely. She cried herself to sleep most nights. She knew she was a failure as a mother. She hadn't been able to protect any of her children.

Generally, parents become aware of drugtaking in a subtle way, picking up signals. Wait until you are certain and then confront the young person calmly with the evidence that something is wrong.

Often family members protect someone who is using because it seems the right thing to do. When someone close behaves in such a way that it protects a young person from the consequences of their drug taking, it is called enabling. When you enable, you are really preventing young persons from seeing the full extent of the damage the drugs is doing to them; you are feeding into their delusion about their drug relationship and helping them to deny the full reality of the harmful consequences of the drug to them, their body, their self-respect, their relationship, their school and work. They want to believe it's 'not that bad', that they are not hurting anyone, 'that I can always change tomorrow or when I want to.' Young people taking drugs do not want to face up to the possibility of permanent damage or serious consequences. When you turn a blind eye to their physical state or clean up after them or make excuses at school or work about them not turning up or write notes about schoolwork not done, you may be helping them to pretend that everything is OK.

CHRIS

Chris's mother knows that he is using drugs. For her it is very obvious. Her husband won't even talk to her about it, he is so angry and upset. 'He's a good-for-nothing. I'm having nothing to do with him any more.' She knows he never did have anything to do with Chris anyway, and so once again she feels on her own. She gives Chris money constantly because she fears that if she refuses him he will go out and rob someone. She'd rather give him money than see him end up in prison. She feels he's had a rough deal all his life, with a father who doesn't care, and she doesn't want Chris to suffer any more. She cleans up his vomit in the bathroom and cleans up his room without a word. Sometimes she asks him to be a good lad and to try to keep on the right road. She knows he loves her and he cries when he has behaved badly and promises he will not do it again. She knows he means it when he says that and she blames the drugs. He can't handle them and she worries that he will get too involved with them. But every time Chris promises her that everything will be OK, she believes him.

Family

Family members and friends end up enabling, protecting the young person, taking responsibility for their chores and duties, covering up for them, lying for them, cleaning up after them, allowing them to continue to abuse them for the best possible reasons. Often they have a sense of loyalty to the young person; they are concerned about the family's good name; they feel personally responsible for the problem or they are tying to change the young person by attempting to control their behaviour. They may be trying to protect the rest of the family, trying to prevent rows and disruption which would upset their partners, parents or other children in the family. They may be afraid of losing the relationship with the young person. Sometimes families have a belief that no one should know their business, that they should be able to deal with their own problems. They may be physically afraid of the young person who may be verbally and physically aggressive. It is difficult to admit even to yourself that you are being abused by your own child.

Every parent I have met feels at some level that somehow it is their fault, that they have failed their children in some way, or treated them wrongly or brought them up badly, and that this is the reason for their problem. Parents in particular have great difficulty in stopping enabling, because they feel somehow responsible, not only for the drugging itself, but also for stopping it. It is difficult to for them to realise that there is no answer to the question why. There has been a great deal of research into the theories of addiction and as yet no one clear factor has emerged to explain why a particular individual becomes addicted. Why does one in a family of twelve become addicted ? Why do three out of a family of three? Why does one family have no addiction, and yet next door does ? Some of the aspects which seem to play a role have already been mentioned; familial attitude to drugs in general, environmental factors like the area in which one lives, some personality difficulties and family crises. However none of these factors are the reasons why someone becomes addicted. Rather it is people's personal relationship with drugs which ensures that they suffer damage and harm. It is their personal commitment that cause the effects the drugs have on them. They become addicted because they love what drugs do to them and only they can change their relationship with drugs. All that family members can do is accept the drug relationship in its full reality, face up to the consequences for the young person and help them accept and face up to addiction also.

Friends

Friends of young people often end up lying for them, covering up for them, saying they are places they aren't and not telling them about their worries for them. Tessa's friends fit into this category. Some of them don't want to look at the situation because that would involve looking at themselves, but some of her older friends who are not themselves using, and who have been dropped by Tessa because they are 'not enough fun' have been distressed about her. They do not challenge her because she jeers them, get angry at them and has been known to physically attack when necessary. They don't tell her parents or their teachers because that would be 'grassing' and they don't want to get her in trouble. They don't know what to do.

The mothers of Chris and Keith feel responsible and their

fear is that they will drive their sons away totally. They believe that if they can hang on to their relationship with their sons, they can support them and stop things getting worse. Unfortunately they fail to realise that the drugs are already corroding their sons' relationship with them, that the drugs are dictating the conditions of the relationship and that they are helping the relationship with the drugs to continue, by supporting the denial that the drugs are the problem. Not the fathers, not themselves, not even their son's personalities. The primary problem here is the drug relationship and until that is faced up to, nothing else can change. Indeed everything will continue to get worse.

Often lack of awareness that addiction is an illness or a disease may lead to families acting in a enabling manner. They may see each event as separate and unconnected and react to each crisis, each symptom of the drug dependency, as another different occasion, rather than seeing the overall picture.

TOM

Tom's parents, Val and Sheila, have been struggling with his disruptive, rude, cold and uninterested behaviour for quite some time. They are baffled by it, and though to others it is quite obvious what the problem is, they have never quite realised that Tom is an alcoholic and drug addict. They have put the numerous rows, breaking of promises and deadlines, lying and secretiveness down to Tom not loving them any more, not wanting them any more, not caring about anything any more. Loudly Val professes Tom to be a criminal, a bad person, without any conscience or heart, morals or standards. He rages and is full of anger that Tom will not listen to him, will not do as he says, will not respect him as head of the household. Inwardly he is very hurt and confused. He loves his three children but Tom is his eldest, his only son, and he always had a special love for him. He took him everywhere, had lots of plans and goals for him, wanted Tom to have everything he didn't have. He wanted him to have a comfortable home, a good education, a good job, a good start in life. Val worked hard every day to provide for his family; he took pride in his home, his wife, his children. Now Tom seemed to be throwing it all away, to have no interest, no respect, no gratitude for what Val had worked hard to provide for him. So Val attempted to teach Tom some lessons. He tried to withhold money, check on his every movement, keep him indoors, refused to let him go to discos and parties, demanded that the rest of the family take his side against Tom and did not give him money or let him out. Of course this just made Tom more defiant and angry. Tom reacted aggressively and abusively, screaming, 'No one is going to treat me like this. How could anyone want to stay in a house like this! It's a prison.'

Tom became progressively more secretive and withdrawn. He felt more hard done by and Val's reactions just gave him a better excuse to get drunk. He was also able to avoid recognising his own personal loss of control over alcohol by justifying his behaviour as 'serving Val right' and 'showing him how bad he really is '. Deep down, Tom also loves Val, as Val loves him, and he believes Val's assertions that he is no good any more. He longs for Val's approval but his relationship with alcohol has taken over and he constantly fails not only Val but also himself. He copes with these failure by focusing on blame, blaming Val and his pressure, and moving more and more towards drinking and drugging companions. When he is drinking, he does not go home, because he is so ashamed he doesn't want Val or Sheila or his sisters to see him.

The rows and quarrels in the home are taking over, and Tom's sisters often feel that Tom is the only person who matters. The conversation day and night seems to be Tom, Tom and more Tom. They feel left out and cheated, that no matter what they do, or how hard they try to please, comfort or cheer up their mum and dad, it's still Tom they're preoccupied with. They reckon Tom knows exactly how to manipulate their mum, always managing to get around her no matter what. The littlest thing he does makes her very grateful. And she believes all his promises and spends her time asking them to mind him, to look out for him, to watch where he's going and what he's doing and who he is with. She keeps telling them not to annoy him and to keep out of his way. That really upsets them: keep out of his way, when he's walking through the house as if he owns it, looking down his nose at everyone, leaving everything lying everywhere, playing loud music and sneering at them! They don't know which is worse: mum licking up to Tom, Tom acting like a pig or dad roaring and screaming at everyone all the time. They weren't doing anything but they were the ones who got the rough end of dad's tongue. Tom always made sure he was gone out of the way.

PATRICK

In Patrick's home there is a also a lot of distress and unhappiness about what is happening. His parents are also all too aware of his drugging. They too have run the whole gamut of experiences: giving money, lending money, having money stolen, mood swings, rudeness, hostility, promises made, promises broken, disappointment, worry fear, anger, hurt. You name it, they've gone through it . When Peggy's sister first asked her if Patrick was using drugs she just laughed, but when a few months later she asked if Patrick was dealing drugs she cried. Peggy and Ted were at their wit's end. They had tried sitting down with Patrick, reasoning with him. They'd dragged him to a counsellor once; they'd cried, begged, pleaded, threatened. They'd got tough with him and called the gardai. They'd forgiven him time and time again, bailed him out of debts when people came to the door, sometimes to the sum of several hundred pounds. They'd paid fines for him, made excuses to the teachers and school for him, did everything they could to support him. Still they had to look on and know their son was lying to them, hiding drugs on them, stealing wherever he could and seemingly doing whatever he wanted. Peggy felt she couldn't go any longer to the local shops, that everyone knew her son was a thief. She knew he'd been shoplifting because a neighbour had seen him and told her. She felt so ashamed when she saw him with his druggie friends. For a long time she and Ted blamed them for dragging Patrick down but they both now recognised that Patrick was the same as them and chose to be with them. Ted couldn't bear to walk down his own street. His shame was unbearable. But that was nothing to the frustration and despair he felt watching Patrick destroy himself and the family.

Sometimes Ted lay in bed at night, knowing that Peggy had cried herself to sleep again because Patrick was missing.

Like most other nights he couldn't sleep, although he felt so tired and worn out he wanted to die. Some nights he planned to kill Patrick, because then their pain would be over. How could he explain what it was like to see that happen to your own son, that you loved him so much you couldn't bear to let him live. One of these nights he thought about killing himself in order to bring Patrick to his senses. When he found himself out of bed on the way to where Peggy hid her sleeping tablets so Patrick couldn't find them, he stopped in sheer horror at what he was doing. That night he decided that it would go no further. It was terrible, heartbreaking that Patrick was destroying his life, but he didn't have to destroy theirs also. Ted thought he was going mad. At that moment he decided that if Patrick wanted to go down the path he was on, he'd have to go on his own, that he wasn't getting back into their home until he decided he wanted help to stop drugging. For the first time in months Ted fell asleep within minutes of getting back into bed.

Sometimes parents like Patrick's parents or Tom's parents get so enmeshed in their children's problems that it starts to run their life, to dictate their moods, feelings and reactions. This doesn't happen just to parents; it can happen to a young person's brother and sisters, friends, anyone close to and concerned with someone who is addicted. One way you can describe it is, that as the young person becomes more and more preoccupied and obsessed with their drugs, their parents become more and more preoccupied and obsessed with them. This can happen whether or not the family realises that they are dealing with addiction. The family and individuals in it lose themselves in their attempts to control the young person's behaviour, and this can lead to them neglecting other relationships, fighting with each other, blaming each other for what is happening, getting angry with themselves and others, feeling depressed, worthless, hopeless, irritable, guilty and overwhelmed. They can't concentrate, can't listen, and are consumed in their search to find an answer, a way to stop the drinking and drugging.

This behaviour in its own way is as unhealthy and destructive as the drugging is to relationships and mental health. The sad fact is it does nothing to stop the addiction. It is normal for parents and family to react to the stress of a young person becoming addicted. This unhealthy way of behaving is a normal reaction born out of an attempt to do the best thing, but it does not work. Yet, Val, Sheila, Ted and Peggy continue to try. What do you expect, you might ask. The question is rather: what else can they do? Ted has found his own answer, but the price may already have been too high. The answer lies in accepting the situation and then letting go.

What you should do when you discover your young person is using drugs often depends on their relationship with drugs, how important they are to them and how much they are prepared or able to let go of them. While the initial reaction may be one of hurt and anger, a blazing row is likely to close down channels of communication which are essential to the long-term solution of the problem. It's important not to over-react if you find that your young person has smoked cannabis or had a drink. The worst this may mean is that they have gone along with the crowd, or have been looking for excitement. At this stage all that may be necessary is to sit down and talk about what is happening. Discuss your feelings about drugs, your fears and worries. Make sure the young person understands the dangers of the drugs he or she is using. Be honest; recognise that some drugs are more dangerous than others but point out the risk of psychological addiction, the uselessness of drugs to solve problems. And listen. Listen to what the young person is saying about themselves and their drug taking. Listen to their words and their body language. Gently prompt them to talk about any issues or worries or problems they have been having. Whether or not there is a dependency problem is a crucial factor that can open or close doors. This is a time when your own relationship with drugs such alcohol and tobacco can come under close scrutiny. It's difficult to talk to your child about the dangers of cigarette smoking if you are a smoker yourself. You can request that they don't use drugs, advise them very strongly against them and you have every right to forbid the use of a drug in your own home, even tobacco.

ANNA

Anna's parents have had the shock of their lives, as has Anna herself. Anna is pregnant. She is totally devastated, depressed and withdrawn. She won't leave her room and is crying all the time. Her parents have been so supportive that she feels even worse. She knows they are disappointed, hurt and angry. But she knows they will stand by her no matter what she wants to do. She feels such a fool, an idiot for messing around with alcohol and drugs. She can't even remember what happened. Of course the one thing they were adamant about was wanting to know who the father was. She dug her heels in about that for a couple of days but soon realised that the hurt of that dishonesty was increasing their pain. They were extremely angry with Chris but went over with her to his house and spoke to Chris and his parents in a calm, matter of fact way. 'We talked it over with Anna and she thought and we agree that Chris has a right and even a responsibility to know where drugs have got him, Anna and now a third, totally innocent person. We know Anna did take the drugs of her own free will but Chris encouraged and supplied them. We believe her when she says that she cares a lot about Chris. We are extremely sad and distressed that this had to happen.' Anna heard herself say to Chris, 'This is my baby. I don't want to have anything more to do with you, at least not while you're drinking or drugging.'

When she went home she cried and cried but she was proud of her parents. She didn't think she'd ever feel proud of herself again.

When a young person is more deeply involved in drugs than just using occasionally, or experimenting, it may be difficult to communicate with them or get a straight answer. They may agree and give promises, or just deny outright any use of the drugs. This stage may last for a long while before a true picture emerges. But if you suspect that a young person is using any drug, even cannabis which you may consider harmless, every day, it is important to take action. Once a drug, any drug, becomes part of a normal everyday life, once a drug becomes central to a young person's coping, that young person needs help. Sometimes you may need help at the initial stages of talking of the young person, from a trusted friend, aunt or uncle, an older brother or sister, a teacher, clergyman or doctor. Any of these may be a person you feel comfortable with and can help stop the situation from becoming the attack which may drive the young person into a corner and into further denials. Remember the young person may be as afraid as you, particularly if there have been bad experiences, or if they have been trying to stop themselves. They may be afraid of withdrawal or of damage to their mind, if, for example, there have been blackouts or flashbacks.

Know what you want to achieve before you start. If it is clear that you are worried about the situation, don't want it to continue and want to support the young person to stop, stick with that. Don't back down or be talked out of it. Remain clear and consistent with what you want.

Getting to the stage of knowing what you want is the most difficult. As we have discussed, often families spend months, even years, denying the seriousness of the situation, hoping it is a condition the young person will grow out of, or that the problem will go away. Overcoming the denial of the drugtaking, starting to look at the overall picture of the young person's behaviour and emotional state, and finally facing the reality of drug-related problems can take a long time. Don't try to do it on your own. Even if you only suspect something, there are people at the other end of a phone who can advise you. Talk to your GP, your local health board, a local addiction counsellor, a treatment centre. They will tell you the steps to take. Even if families already know there is definitely a drug problem they will hesitate about talking to anyone or asking for help. Sometimes this is out of fear of rocking the boat, making matters worse, out of shame or out of ignorance. But this is what they need to do.

Another place you can get help to work out what you want from the young person is through joining a support group and meeting people who have faced the same problem. Families Anonymous and Narcotics Anonymous are the two organisations that help families of drug users. This is one of the best ways you can help yourself break the habit of unhelpful and enabling behaviours. The emphasis in these self-support groups is on freeing yourself to listen to your feelings and freeing yourself so as not to feel responsible for the young person's drugtaking. You cannot stop them anyway. If young people want to use, they will find a way.

You need to intervene, to create a situation where they can be helped to understand the damage drugs are doing to them and to find reasons not to use them.

Sometimes crisis occurs naturally as it has for Tessa and her parents and for Anna and Chris. These are opportunities for those involved in a caring manner point out the consequences of drugs and to ask for a commitment to stop. Often a young person will believe and promise that they can stop. If this undertaking is broken, a further crisis occurs which can enable you to move further toward your goal: the young person accepting help to deal with the drug relationship.

KEITH

Keith's mother has been forced into a crisis also, a very frightening and horrific one for the whole family. Ben went into Keith's room late one night to borrow a torch and discovered Keith unconscious. He had accidentally overdosed. Ben woke his mother who phoned for an ambulance and Ben, who had luckily done his first-aid in the scouts, knew what else to do. He

- Checked that Keith was breathing
- Knelt at his side
- Held his chin, gently tilting the head back and opening his airway
- Put Keith in the recovery position. Turned his head towards him
- Straightened his legs, brought his arm across his chest and placed the palm on the floor
- Placed the other arm under his buttock
- Turned Keith towards him, pulling his upper leg towards him
- Readjusted his arm so that his palm was flat beside his head.
  Keith was now lying on his side.
- Ben made sure he could still breathe by tilting his head back
- He kept Keith's knee and hip at right angles to his body.

Ben probably saved Keith's life, in more ways than one,

because that occasion brought an opportunity for Keith to be detoxed and to think about what drugs were doing to himself and his family.

But changing behaviour is not easy. Addiction doesn't happen with one puff of a joint. Often young people have tried but failed to keep promises to themselves and their families. The key word is support:

- Look for support for yourself—from family, friends, professionals, support groups.
- Offer support to the young person.
- Organise support for them.

This can range from attendance at Alcoholics Anonymous or Narcotics Anonymous, to medical supervision for detoxification with a general practitioner, a local drug unit or a hospital, to assessment by an addiction counsellor, to individual or group counselling as an outpatient or inpatient at a treatment centre, health clinic or hospital.

Remember the young person who is addicted is unable to stop without support; that is intervention. They are out of control whether they are admitting that or not. They are not continuing to use drugs because they are bad but because they are addicted. This does not mean that they are capable of caring at that point. Often they are not and do not care about you or themselves. This is the true horror of addiction; the loss of self, of values, of human emotions like compassion, empathy and concern. This does not mean that a young person is necessarily a lost cause. If they are hurting enough, and you are still prepared to support them to get well, they may let you.

Chapter Nine

Recovery

Admitting the problem is the first step, but it is only the first step. When young people begin to admit that they are in trouble, that they are worried or frightened, then comes the possibility of supporting them in what is a long, hard, though rewarding. struggle.

First, they need to recognise the extent of their relationship with drugs. Often addicted young people will focus on one particular drug as their problem and want to hold on to others.

KEITH

For example, Keith has used opiates, but even if an overdose of Napps has caused his crisis, he needs to look at his relationship with alcohol and cannabis and his use of sleeping tablets. He needs to trace his relationship with drugs from the onset and begin to see how his drug relationship dictated all his choices, his use of time and energy and money, his chase after the high, his dropping of friends and hobbies and interests if they didn't fit in, his neglect of schoolwork, his choice of places to go, his change in attitude towards his family, his mood swings and negative attitudes like self-pity, anger and resentment towards people close to him including his mum and Ben. He will then realise how they kept his drinking and drugging right on course. He will not be able to do this on his own, because delusion has set in. This enables Keith to go on using his drink and drugs. This is a difficult thing for Keith to grasp—that it is not only what *might* happen to his body and mind, but what has already happened. His defences have set up a whole complicated support system for his drugging lined with row after row of minimisations, excuses, justifications and reasons why what he did was not so bad, not all the time, not any different from other people, not as bad as many others only this drug and not that drug, because everyone else did it, because he deserved it, because he worked so hard, because his father deserted them, because so much was expected from him, because no one cared how he felt, because he needed something to keep him going, because he needed something to live for, because he couldn't help it, because he didn't know what he was doing, because it wasn't him but the alcohol or the drugs, but he knew and was ashamed, but he knew and was sorry, but he knew all about what it was like for his mother and family, but he knew all about what it was like for him, and he wouldn't do it again, he promised.

He needs to have all these defences, excuses, reasons and protestations that he now knows what it is all about, exposed for what they are—defences. If he is allowed to believe that he has a handle on his addiction and that admitting there is a problem and then being physically detoxified or brought safely off the drugs until there are no withdrawal symptoms, is enough, then he is likely to run into big problems. He needs support to recognise his addiction, that is the overpowering psychological need to use drugs which has taken over his mind and limited his emotional development. Keith at the moment is a Keith who needs to drink and drug. His way of thinking, of relating to others, of dealing with emotions, have all become drug-centred. This is very difficult and scary to grasp. But Keith needs to be aware of the way drugs have affected him. This is what accepting your addiction is about, looking at how the drug relationship has changed you. It is not enough just to admit that drugs are causing problems.

Fellowship
This is where Narcotics Anonymous, Alcoholics Anonymous, addiction counsellors and drug and alcohol treatment centres can help a young person. At the other end of the phone is experienced support, be it professional or experiential. A young person can avail of both; he or she stands little chance of making it alone. At the very least they need the kindness, care, concern and strength of those people who know exactly what they are going through because they have been there themselves. Recovering drug addicts and alcoholics also know the pitfalls, the lies you can tell yourself, the shortcuts you can try to take, the ways out you can provide for yourself. Wisdom, experience and support are there every night at AA or NA meetings. Members will offer to fellowship young

people and help them along the way. But it takes a willingness, a desire to get well on the part of young addicts.

The first step is: 'We admitted we are powerless over alcohol and drugs and that our lives had become unmanageable '.

Recognition that there is a problem, realisation that you can't do it on your own, willingness to take help, to trust the process, to listen to advice, to make changes and be open to hear others points of view and feelings about issues, are essential. This includes being open to listen to and communicate with, family and friends, not only counsellors and members of the fellowships. Often, in fact usually, relationships with important people in your life are damaged, at least confused and hurt. Your family may be angry with you. You need to listen to how it has been for them, because this will help you to grasp how drugs have affected you. Usually treatment centres can help your family and yourself to talk about these issues. Family therapy is another option, often available from your health board, addiction counsellors, child guidance clinics or private therapy centres.

Addiction is a family illness. Because parents and family members have suffered and been affected by the drugging behaviour, so they too have had to find ways of coping with the situation. As we have seen, ways of coping can bring their own problems and cause damage to relationships. It is equally important that parents and family members seek help and support for themselves. Again the fellowships of Families Anonymous and Nar-Anon have an enormous amount of wisdom and help to offer. Their phone number is in every phone book, no matter where you live. This is the best way you can support a young person to recover, by looking after yourself and learning how to support recovery. Similarly, individual counselling and family therapy can help family members to recover.

Detachment
Family and parents need to learn how to detach. This does not mean they don't care. It simply means that they can learn how to let go, to detach from the young person, in love. Ted found his way to let go of Patrick. It wasn't that he stopped loving or caring but that he realised that Patrick needed to see

the consequences of his drugging in order to recognise that he was in trouble and needed help. Detachment is based on the realisation that each person is responsible for his or her self, that we can't solve problems that aren't ours to solve and that worrying doesn't help. This may be particularly hard if we are dealing with young children, especially if they are your children. Parenting is about letting our children become independent, even pushing them to become independent when they are forcing us to keep looking after them. Addiction is about dependency. When young people become dependent on drugs, one of the consequences is that they become more and more irresponsible, depending more on others to look after them, do their chores or work, to pick up the pieces, to mend their mess. It is tempting for parents to continue that which they have done throughout their child's life. It may be heartbreaking to know your child is making mistakes. Detachment means allowing young people to be who they are. It is giving them the freedom to be responsible and to grow, and giving yourself the same freedom to live your own life. In the fellowships they use the serenity prayer as a constant reminder of this principle

God grant me the serenity to accept the things I cannot change, the courage to change the things I can and the wisdom to know the difference.

Detachment involves living in the present and not trying to control everything. It involves accepting reality. When parent detach, they free young people to begin to solve their own problems. It is important not to detach in anger. There is no advantage to a parent of a young person in trouble with drugs if the door is shut on them, if they are told to get out and not come back and rejected in anger. Young people need to be clear what is happening. They need to know that you are not going to help them kill themselves with drugs, that you are not going to protect them from the consequences, that you are not going to allow them to abuse their home and family either by using drugs in the home or by subjecting the family to drug-related problems, that you are going to protect other members of the family from the drugs even if you can't protect the abusers. They need to know that you are still there for them, that you care for them, that it is the drugs you disapprove of and that if they want help to deal with their drug relationship you will support them.

For some parents it is much like shutting the door completely to ask a young person to leave. No one can tell you what to do. Ultimately, remember, no one has the right to tell you what to do. Always follow your instinct; do what feels right for you. If you are doing the basic things, being honest about the problem and seeking support for yourself, you will gradually find the answers that are right for you, by yourself. The answers lie in acceptance of the problem for what it is and in its full reality. But change, even positive change may be difficult and painful. Moving forward is always a loss, a loss of the past, of what was. The need for progression towards acceptance is the same for all change, whether it is your child's addiction, your own addiction, a new house, a death, a loss of a job. Elizabeth Kubler-Ross identified it as a grief process, and named five stages:

First you go into *denial*. This is a state of shock, numbness, a refusal to face up to the truth. When young people are first asked to look at their drug relationship, their first stage is also denial. They refuse to look at the damage their drugs are doing to them and their lives. They insist they can handle it, that it's not that bad, they didn't take that much and so on. Their emotions are flat, detached, even non-existent. Recovery from their addiction will require grieving. At this stage young addicts really believe the lies they tell themselves; it is a stage of sincere delusion.

Family members may also be initially in a stage of denial, when they first start to become aware of the drugging. They shut out the fact from their mind, forget events, don't put two and two together. This process of denial is a normal process, a safety valve by which we stop our emotions becoming overloaded. It is an attempt to prevent anxiety.

The second stage is *anger*. Young addicts become very upset, angry, annoyed at facing up to their addiction. They don't like what they are hearing. It hurts to hear things that they have put a lot of energy into hiding, and they often get angry at everyone around for exposing them, unmasking them, for robbing them of their dream, their haven. Because drugs have been their attempt to seek oblivion or to seek happiness, when they are asked to look at the true picture, their loss is great, their pain is great and so often their anger is great.

Similarly when parents start to see the true picture, they too feel vulnerable. Perhaps they feel somewhat fooled by the lies and deceptions and also angry at the loss of their 'innocence'.

Then the stage of *bargaining* is reached. The individual tries to come up with a plan that will make things better. 'If I go for treatment, they'll get off my back'; 'If I give up drugs for a year I'll be better able to handle them'; 'If I can drink I'll give up my drugs.'

The families of the young person often resort to bargaining as well. 'If you protect my daughter I'll donate to St Vincent de Paul every month.'; 'If I clean his room once a week he'll be nicer to us.' (This was Ben, Keith's brother). 'If his father would speak to him politely once in a while, he wouldn't drug again.'

The fourth stage is *depression*. This is when reality hits home, when all our worst fears are realised. For the young addict who is facing up to the loss of his drugs, this is the point at which he realises that he has thrown a lot away to continue drugging and that he has become trapped by it.

Parents reach this stage when they feel they cannot go on. Ted began to reach for oblivion for himself at this stage, to have a death wish. It was at this point that he reached the final stage of *acceptance*. This is when an individual stops struggling and accepts the reality of the situation. It may not be a happy realisation but there is peace in realising that the struggle is over, that all that can be done is to accept the situation for what it is, in all its aspects, and learn to live with it. The individual stops running and hiding from the truth.

When young people truly accept their addiction they have to learn to live with their dependency, to be aware of its impact and devise a way to cope with life without drugs. This can be difficult because it means accepting a major loss in their life. Their drugs have become their reality, their focus, their reason for living. If you can imagine our life like a moulded tray with different compartments and sections for each aspect of life, there would be a section for school, one for music, one for football and so on. There would also be one for drugs and one for alcohol. Each person's tray is filled differently with different quantities in all sections. The drug section may be empty for some people. When young people becomes addicted this section is filled to overflowing and it starts to invade other sections also, pushing out what's in them. When the tray is emptied of drugs, we find a lot of gaps, a big empty space. This is very painful for young people. Often their drugs involve not just the taking of drugs, the buzz they get from them, but also the fact that drugs give them an image, an identity. They love the whole ritual of the drug-taking, the places and people, the being in the know. As in any other group, there is a pecking order among drug abusers, a hierarchy. As young people move more and more into drugs, more and more into addiction, sadly they move higher up the perking order. They have arrived. They are like part of a secret illicit organisation. This also gives the high of the excitement of sharing in something not only together, but against others. From the early days when young teenagers go drinking in fields and empty houses, or sniffing gas, glue or paint thinners at the back of a garage or church, part of the bonding is due to there being a danger of being caught, a group together against the gardai or whoever.

This sense of belonging is difficult to let go of because it involves standing on your own and being mature enough to make your own decisions. Old drug companions will jeer and mock; they are threatened by anyone who questions the group, and they will do their best to entice a young user back into the fold in order to quiet their own uneasiness. It is also a sad event to lose friends of perhaps several or many years duration, even if they are drug users. Mostly the relationships within the drug culture remain very superficial, with drugs being the only thing in common, the only activity, the only conversation. Sometimes, though, young people have moved into drugs together and it is both a frightening and sad experience for young recovering addicts to leave their pals behind, to step out alone into a world they do not know. They now have to face the many tasks of maturing adulthood without the comfort zone and escape route of drugs. For example, Frank loves the rave scene, He knows a lot of people who belong to that scene and lives for the weekend. He loves the people, the music, the clothes, the feeling, the excitement, the whole atmosphere. For him, to give up drugs is to give up more than just the substances. Though he is abusing drugs, he still sees the drug culture as a social scene.

Many young addicts face this loneliness and emptiness. They feel isolated in their recovery. Accepting the reality and seriousness of their drug relationship leaves them bereaved and fearful. If alcohol is a problem this may also be particularly acute. Like Ecstasy, alcohol provides a meeting point, a shared experience, not only for a select few, but also for the majority of both young and older people in this culture. In the early stages of recovery young people need to avoid places and people they associate with using drugs. This helps them to deal with the compulsion to use the pub, the dance-club. These maintain sufficient emotional triggers for the young person even to begin to feel high, and certainly to trigger euphoric memories and the desire for that high.

When young people realise they should avoid these places it often feels like they are being asked to give up their youth. 'Where can I go?' they think. 'What can I do?'; ' How can I meet anyone?'; 'Does this mean I can have no fun any more?'.

Young people need support and comfort and the sensitivity of family to understand these difficulties not just in returning to life, but in belatedly trying to build one. Because of the crucial period of time in which they have used drugs, young people have delayed their developmental tasks, and recovery involves the task of facing them and working through them.

For family members the acceptance that a young person is out of their control, that the young person's addiction has rendered them powerless in the situation can be a release in some way, but it also can be very frightening and sad.

PEGGY

For Peggy, Ted's decision to put Patrick out of the house was one of the most difficult periods, even though she totally agreed. She knew that they weren't helping Patrick the way things were, and like Ted, she was desperate to change the situation, to make Patrick stop. For her his leaving the house was a last attempt to control, to try to make Patrick change. She aged fifteen years in the last year, worn down by the worry and sorrow of the situation and also exhausted by the constant turmoil. She had at last succumbed to the lure of tranquillisers and sleeping tablets, living each day in her own induced drug-like dream. She had found Patrick injecting in the bathroom one day, and the sight had frozen the blood in her veins. There he was, her son, sitting on the edge of the bath, a belt around his arm and a syringe hanging from his vein. His eyes were half closed and he looked like all the images of a junkie. And this her son, her little boy, destroying himself in her bathroom. She knew Ted was right. but in the first few weeks, even months of Patrick's living rough, she walked the streets and fields, looking for him, just hoping for a glimpse of his face, to know that he was still alive for another day. She'd look constantly into the faces of all the other young users who hung around Patrick's spots and wonder did they know him, did their parents feel like herself and Ted. Peggy's friends were horrified at the determination in her; she'd lie in bed at night wondering if he was all right. Would he be cold, did he have anything to eat, would someone hurt him, physically or sexually? Every now and then she'd get a note in the door from Patrick asking could he come home. When she'd meet him down the street, filthy dirty, she'd feel sure what she wanted. 'Please come home, but you must give up the drugs.' It took six months but one day Patrick arrived at the door. 'I want to give them up, mum.'

When young people moves into recovery they need support to grow up, become more independent, find ways to meet their own emotional needs, learn how to deal with their feelings, how to communicate and express their emotions, how to assert themselves rather than act aggressively or feel helpless. They need support to get to know who they are, to find out their strengths as well as their weaknesses, to get to like, respect and even love themselves. Recovery for any addict is a difficult and vulnerable period but this is particularly true for adolescents and young adults. They have not had the chance to build up relationships, standards, a way of life or a job or career to work back to. They have not even got memories of life before drugs to remind them of what recovery can bring. They are face to face with all the anxieties and fears they started out with. Life is still an unknown quantity to them. Not only do they need help to remove the denial and defensive thinking that created the delusionary state which supported their drug taking, they need a safe place to nurture their ability to talk about their feelings, their desires, fears, anxieties, disappointments. By this means they can find a different way of coping with the huge task of becoming a mature adult, other than by opting out. Many young people have very real issues to deal with other than their drug-taking, issues which they tried to avoid by losing themselves in addiction.

Loss of a parent through death, separation, divorce, addiction is one situation the young person may have a whole range feelings about. Physical abuse, emotional abuse, sexual abuse are all possible areas that a young person in recovery may need to deal with. Difficulties in school, failures to cope with the academic demands of the educational system, sexual confusion and sexual difficulties, loneliness, lack of social skills are just a few of the situations young people face when they stop taking drugs. Unless they receive support through the fellowships and counselling, through individual work and group work, within their family and from friends their likelihood of returning to drugs is high. Addiction is an emotional illness; it is the reliance on a chemical to deal with feelings and emotions. If we just remove the drugs, the young person is left with an empty space, as their way of coping has been taken away. Something has to replace it or they will believe they need to drug in order to cope with their feelings. The more uncomfortable feelings, unresolved issues and feelings of fear, anxiety, hurt, resentment, bitterness and anger the young person has, the more vulnerable they are.

Acceptance needs to include not only acceptance of their addiction but also the ability to accept themselves as they are, to live in the present and to enjoy life. Initially recovery is a state of deprivation. If it remains that, relapse to drug taking will quickly follow. The issues in their life have not caused the addiction, but the young person's inability to cope with them, to deal with and express their feelings, may have created a need which the drugs filled. These uncomfortable feelings may have made drug euphoria very attractive. Often the avoidance, denial of issues and lack of ability to communicate and express your feelings may be a family pattern. This serves to underline the need for all family members, including parents, to seek support to deal with feelings past and present, and to learn how to relate differently to the young person in order to support their new life. Aftercare groups in treatment centres aim to support young addicts and their parents for the first year or two in recovery. It is not enough for a young person to retreat into the family. They need to work towards independence, material and emotional, to take responsibility for their sexual and social lives, to develop a career, develop friendships and make personal choices about how they want to lead their lives. They need to do this without the crutch of drugs and to find out who they really are. If they do not like themselves, either because of hurts in the past or because of their drugging experiences, this can be painful and difficult unless they are supported.

On the other hand, young people will experience great clarity of thought and feelings without drugs. Their youthful energy, health and exuberance will be recovered and these will empower them greatly.

Chapter Ten

Prevention

Children's Bill of Rights

For every child, understanding and the guarding of his personality as his most precious gift.

For every child, a home and that love and environment, harmonious and enriching, free from conditions which tend to thwart his development.

For every child, a community which recognises and plans for his needs and protects him against physical danger, moral hazard and disease.

For every child, such teaching and training as will prepare him for successful parenthood and, for parents, supplementary training to fit them to deal wisely with the problems of parenthood.

The task of growing up is a huge one. During adolescence and young adulthood, young people are starting to explore a new world in a new way. There are many pressures on them to become successful and independent, to have new relationships and find new goals. How can parents and concerned adults best create an atmosphere in which young people can negotiate their tasks? There must be safety, but in a way that preserves young people's dignity and nurtures their freedom to choose for themselves, while giving them guidelines which will help them.

Patience, consistency and communication are three of the essential elements parents need to develop in order to support their young people. Parents often meet this stage in their children's life with their own preset ideas and horror stories from their own youth. They may be determined that it will not be the same as it was for them, either because they know the dangers or because they felt suffocated or controlled themselves. It is important for both parents and children to develop positive images of this time in their life. This is a good exciting period with lots of energy around. The hope is that the energy can be channelled positively.

1 Make your children feel good about themselves. Praise their efforts, their accomplishments. Tell them what you like about them or about young people in general. Focus on the energy for change, the idealism, the creativity of adolescence. Recognise the difficulties young people are facing, try to recognise behaviour as experimental and to value the growth that it represents. When they won't sit still, admire their energy. When they want to wear 'weird' clothes and 'bizarre' hairstyles, admire their courage. Be aware of your own wounds; get support for yourself to deal with your own regrets, losses and unfulfilled dreams. When you are hurting it is difficult to deal with your teenager's pain or fear. Remember that all children are different and accept them. Help them to find something they are good at and show your pride in their achievements, be it amusing the family, cooking great cheese on toast, or making a shopping trip memorable ! Everyone thrives on success. Life can be difficult for young peopls who believe that they do not fit the image or dreams their parents have had for them. Let young people know you value them for who they are and what they do, rather than what you would like them to be or do. This is an easy trap for parents to fall into when they love their children and want what they consider the best for them. Some children may fit into that role; others may not. It is important that a young person does not feel rejected, or 'less' than another sibling, who is really only different, not brighter or more confident.

2 Talk to your children. It is essential to keep talking and keep listening. Give them your full attention. Turn off the television, stop reading the paper. Yes, they always pick the most inconvenient moment, like when you're in the middle of making the dinner or just stepping into the bath or in a rush out somewhere. But be ready to respond; you may not get a second chance. Ask for their opinion and advice, listen to it and respect it even if you don't agree. Keep an open mind about their ideas, and hear them out. Do not dismiss them just because you feel differently. Talk about feelings as well as facts, talk about yourself, your feelings. Treat them like human beings. They have a lot in common with adults, even if they look different. You don't always have to protect young

people from decisions or family crises. There are hidden agendas and secrets. Be a good role model in communication as well as other ways. Provide a forum, a meeting point for all the family. Days can go by when everyone is rushing out to school and work at different times, all going out to games or social occasions and passing each other by except for five minutes here and five minutes there. The ritual of Sunday lunch as a meeting time has a lot to be said for it, or it can be a particular night as a family night.

Young people have strong views, so it is important not to resort to sarcasm, teasing or jeering. The more communication is the norm in your home the more support young people have to express their feelings, fears and anxieties. If they are getting into difficulties, becoming secretive, withdrawn or uncommunicative, it will be more noticeable.

3 Really listen to your children. Get to know them; let them see that you are there for them, that they can confide in you safely and without fear of censure or rejection. When there are disagreements or grievances, listen. Sit down and talk about it. Negotiate with young people rather than resorting to 'It's no because I say so.' This mean both sides have to give a little. Young people find it difficult to compromise; they want all or nothing. This is good learning for them. Allow young people then to be involved in the decision-making process in the home. When you want to make a point bargain or bribe with good things, for example, 'I'll not rag you about your room if you...' Remember to be consistent, to stick to your decisions and to explain your actions and feelings, thoughts and decisions. This helps young people to feel they are being treated as equals. When you give a little, you show you're prepared to consider their point of view and that you do not just assume that you know what's best for them. This allows young people to feel good about themselves and believe they are worthwhile and so have something to offer. It helps if you recognise and try to remember that a lot of dissension is not just rebellion for the sake of aggravation, but young people trying to stand on their own. Don't push your opinion on them; try and lead them into drawing their own conclusions. Then you can reinforce the fact that it is their own decision.

4 Be a good role model. Your attitudes towards alcohol and drugs affects young people more than anything you can say. Maybe you need to question and reassess your own habits and patterns of using all drugs from tobacco to prescribed drugs to alcohol. Remember illegal drugs are only part of the picture.

5 Make family rules. It is important to be tolerant when working with and relating to young people. They need space and freedom to experiment but this does not mean that anything goes. Although young people can and will challenge you all the way, they feel safest when working within limits, when they know how far they can go. Every family has rules, even if you think yours hasn't. Many of them are unspoken rules, or rules that have developed over the years and everyone knows about: for example don't talk when your father is listening to the news. Sometimes we think that everyone knows the rules of the family: 'Don't you know the rule about leaving the bathroom clean and dry after you?' Of course everybody doesn't always know the rules, as evidenced by the fact that this question is usually asked when someone is not keeping the rules. Usually Harry has worked out the rules as being, 'Clean and dry the bathroom when mum is around, because then you will be made to do it anyway. If not it's OK.' The rules of a family are the factors that make it possible for members to live together reasonably calmly and contentedly. They are a form of shorthand, and looking at the rules in your family is reading the shorthand of the values and standards your family live by. Sitting down as a family and talking about rules is a good way to find out which ones are actually in force. Then you can find out which are appropriate, which are understood, which are being kept or not, which are unfair, and which are missing.

There are often rules about feelings in a family, such as, 'You mustn't feel that way.' There may also be rules about affection or the showing of affection, such as: 'It's okay to hug and kiss your mum until you are twelve years old.' 'After nine years of age you don't kiss your brother.' 'Dads are not for showing affection to, except if you're a girl.' Often family rules include taboos about sex: 'You don't talk about that!' There are rules about the age at which you can do certain activities . And so on an so on.

If the rules in your family can be changed, the family can grow and modify itself to accommodate the members, their development and growth. Throw out obsolete ones, introduce new ones. Rules can be made about drugs and drug related behaviour. When you are setting limits, decide what matters, what can cause a real danger, and what is intolerable to the other family members. Set limits that are realistic as well as reasonable, for example, smoking in the young person's room only or in the garden. If an issue isn't really important, let it go. Be willing to discuss issues, to compromise or to change your mind if it's appropriate. Be flexible. But do not be nagged or bullied. If teenagers get their own way they tend to try harder to do so next time.

6 Help your children to develop strong values. Teach your children by example to think about what they say and do. Taking a value system seriously and behaving in accordance with it can help your child to say 'no' for him- or herself. Reward them for good behaviour; comment on what you liked. Thank them when they've behaved in a way you feel proud of. Praise them when they have achieved something. Behaviour that gets attention tends to be repeated.

7 Help your children to deal with peer pressure: teach them how to be assertive, to be their own person by giving them the right to talk directly and honestly about their feelings, thoughts and requests, by talking directly and honestly about your own feelings and asking directly what you want. Young people will then learn that it's OK to have their own feelings and thoughts, but that others do not necessarily have to agree.

Encourage your children to bring friends home and make their friends welcome. Don't forbid friends just because you don't like them; instead, make an effort to get to know them. If you are still worried or anxious, talk to your children about it, then trust their judgement. It is important for young people to have friends, to belong. If they are supported in creating a circle of friends for themselves they are less likely to feel lonely, vulnerable, worthless or inadequate, and will be better able to think and act for themselves and resist unhealthy peer pressure.

8 Encourage healthy, creative activities. Young people need constant stimulation, interesting ways of using up their excess energy and enthusiasm. Boredom can lead to drugging.

9 Educate your children about the danger of drug use.

10 Know what to do if you suspect a problem . Look out for symptoms and telltale signs. Inform yourself about where to get help.

This is probably a blueprint for a perfect world. People being people and both parents and children being human, life in a family does not run smoothly. The big question is whether your home is a good place to live, where people are happy, where self-worth is high, communication is direct, clear and honest, rules are flexible and there are choices for family members. If these conditions apply, then the family is a nurturing one. Mistakes can still happen, problems do arise, but these can usually be worked through. Any troubled family can become a nurturing, happy one. The first step is to accept the reality that your family is a troubled one. Forgive yourself for your mistakes and give your family and yourself permission to change. Take action. Do something different.

Your questions may still be unanswered when you reach the end of this book. What will happen? Will it be OK? What will happen to John, Tom, Anna, Alice, Keith, Chris, Patrick and Sam (to name a few)? I believe in happy endings. I think everyone is entitled to a happy ending. Every day in my work with addicted people I see the possibility and actuality of happy endings. With courage your story will have a happy ending also.

God bless.

Recommended Reading

Beattie, M. *Co-dependent No More*, Hazelden.

Blaze-Gordon, T. (1987). *Drug Abuse*, David and Charles.

Department of Health. Health Promotion Unit.

Department of Health. (1986). *Directory of Organisations Concerned with Substance Abuse*.

Ditzler & Ditzler (1987). *Coming off Drink*, Papermac.

Ditzler, Ditzler and Haddon (1986). *Coming off Drugs*, Papermac.

Cumberton, J. (1982). *Drugs and Young People*, Ward River Press.

Fenwick, E. and Smith, Dr. T. (1993). *Adolescence: The Survival Guide for Parents and Teenagers*, Dorling Kindersley.

Golden Pages Ltd. (1991) *Directory of Alcoholic and Drug Services in the Republic of Ireland*.

IAC. (1991). Directory of Counselling.

Leigh, V. (1988). *Drugs, Why say no?*, Penguin.

Maxwell, R. (1987). *The Booze Battle*, Ballantine.

Rhodes and Jason (1988). *Preventing Substance Abuse in Children and Adolescents*, Pergamon.

Roche, H. (1990). *The Addiction Process*, HCI.

Satir, V. (1988). *The New Peoplemaking*, Science and Behaviour Books.

Rimoff and Carper, S. (1992). *How to tell if your kids are using 'drugs'*, Facts on File.

Stockley, D. (1992) *Drug Warning*, Optima.

Trickett, S. (1986) *Coming Off*, Thorson.

Ward, Y. (1993). *A Bottle in the Cupboard: Women and Alcohol*, Attic Press.

Useful Addresses

'A' Bar Dublin Central Mission
c/o Social Aid Centre
Lower Abbey Street, Dublin 1
Tel (01) 8740691/8742123

Addiction Information Service
9B Farmhill Road
Goatstown, Dublin 14
Tel (01) 2988983

Alcohol and Drug Abuse
Treatment Centre, Arbour House
Douglas Road, Cork
Tel (021) 968933

Alcohol and Drug Counselling
Services, 1 Cook Terrace
Portlaoise, Co. Laois
Tel (0502) 21634 Ext 409

Alcoholism Unit
St Brigid's Hospital
Ballinasloe, Co. Galway
Tel (0905) 42117

Alcohol Treatment Unit
Baggot St. Community
Hospital, 18 Upper Baggot St
Dublin 2
Tel (01) 6607838

Alcoholic Rehabilitation
Centre, Goldenbridge House
Tyrconnell Street,
Inchicore, Dublin 8
Tel (01) 543793/538941
Fax (01) 538941

Ana Liffey Drug Project
13 Lr Abbey Street, Dublin 1
Tel (01) 8786828/8786899

Anawin Community
Drumbarron, Inver Post Office
Co. Donegal
Tel (073) 36063

Ballymun Youth Action Project
1a Balcurris Road, Ballymun
Dublin 11
Tel (01) 8428071

Belmont Hospital, Waterford
Tel (051) 32211

CADHQ
(Community Awareness of Drugs)
6 Excheqer Street, Dublin 2
Tel (01) 6792681

Catholic Social Service Conference
Drugs Awareness Programme
The Red House, Clonliffe College
Dublin 3
Tel (01) 8360011

Coolemine Therapeutic
Community, Coolemine House
19 Lord Edward Street, Dublin 2
Tel (01) 6793765/6794822

Community Addiction
Counselling
see Health Centres
(telephone directory)

Community Addiction Counselling

Health Centre,
Patrick Street
Dun Laoghaire
Tel (01) 2808471/2841169
37 Castle Street, Dublin 2
Tel (01) 4757837

St Andrew's Community Centre
Rialto
Tel (01) 4540021/4531638

Health Centre, Main Street
Tallaght
Dublin 24
Tel (01) 4515397/4515764

Cherry Orchard Hospital
Dublin 10
Tel (01) 6268101

Community Care Office
Rathdown Road, Dublin 7
Tel (01) 389326
(Monday 9am-12pm)

Health Centre, Shopping Centre
Ballymun, Dublin 11
Tel (01) 8420011

Edenmore Health Centre
Edenmore Park, Raheny, Dublin 5
Tel (01) 8480666

Poplar Houe
Naas, Co. Kildare
Tel (045) 76001

HQ 19 Haddington Road
Dublin 4
Clinics: Ashling, Cherry Orchard
Dublin 10
Tel (01) 6602149
Aisling (01) 6232200

Community Alcohol Services
Glen Abbey Centre, Belgard Road
Tallaght, Dublin 24
Tel (01) 516589/516754

Cuan Mhuire
Milltown, Athy, Co. Kildare
Tel (0507) 31090/31493
or
Newry, Co. Down
Tel (080693) 69121

Drug Squad, Harcourt Square
Harcourt Street, Dublin 2
Tel Dublin (01) 8751356/ 8732222
Cork (021) 273161
Limerick (061) 414222

Drug Treatment Centre Board
Trinity Court, 30-31 Pearse St
Dublin 2
Tel (01) 6771122

Dublin Counselling and Therapy
Centre, 18 Haroldville Avenue
SCR, Dublin 8
Tel (01) 4530666

Families Anonymous
(See Telephone Directory)

Health Promotion Unit
Department of Health
Hawkins House, Dublin 2
Tel (01) 6714711

Talbot Centre
29 Upper Buckingham Street
Dublin 1
Tel (01) 8363464

Insitiute for the Study of
Drug Dependence
National Helpline
Tel 01 6771122
9.30am–4.45pm, Monday to Friday
10.30am–12.30pm
Saturday and Sundays
James St Hospital
(AIDs/HIV)

Mater Dei Counselling Centre
Mater Dei Institute
Clonliffe Road, Dublin 3
Tel (01) 8371892

Merchants Quay Project
4 Merchants Quay, Dublin 8
Tel (01) 6790044/6771128

Midland Health Board
Central Office, Arden Road
Tullamore, Co. Offaly
Tel (0506) 21868
Helpline (044) 42144
(0502) 22699

Narcotics Anonymous
(See Telephone Directory)

National Youth Council of Ireland
3 Montague Street, Dublin 2
Tel (01) 4784122/4784407

North Eastern Health Board
St Davnet's Hospital, Monaghan
Tel (047) 81822

Rutland Centre Ltd
KnocklyonHouse
Knocklyon Road Templeogue,
Dublin 16
Tel (01)4946358/4946761/4946972

St John of God Hospital
Stillorgan, Co. Dublin
Tel (01) 2881781

St Patrick's Hospital
Steeven's Lane, James's Street
Dublin 8
Tel (01) 6775432

St John of God Hospital
Stillorgan
Co. Dublin
Tel (01) 2881781

South Eastern Health Board
Carlow/Kilkenny
Dr Connolly (056) 21208
St. Brigid's Hospital
Ballinasloe, Co. Galway
Tel (0905) 42117/42313/42403

St Conal's Hospital
Letterkenny, Co. Donegal
(074) 21022

St Columba's Hospital
Ballytivan, Sligo
Tel (071) 2111

Teen Challenge
4 Beresford Place
Dublin 1
Tel (01) 8786327

Teen Counselling
37 Greenford Gardens,
Quarryvale
Clondalkin
Dublin 22
Tel (01) 6231398

The Cluain Mhuire Service
Newtownpark Avenue
Blackrock, Co. Dublin
Tel (01) 2833766

The Talbot Centre
29 Upper Buckingham Street
Dublin 1
Tel (01) 8363434

Trinity Court
30-33 Pearse Street
Dublin 2
Tel (01) 6771122

Waterford Drug Abuse Resource
Group
c/o South Eastern Health Board
32 The Mall, Waterford

NORTHERN IRELAND
Central Office of AA
152 Lisburn Road
Belfast BT9 6AJ
Tel (0232) 681084 (office hours)

Families Anonymous
in local area telephone directory

Narcotics Anonymous
in local area telephone directory

Northern Ireland Council for
Voluntary Action
127 Ormeau Road
Belfast BT7 1SH
Tel (0232) 321224

Northern Ireland Regional Unit
Shaftsbury Square Hospital
116-122 Great Victoria Street
Belfast BT2 7B6
Tel (0232) 329808

BRITAIN
ADFAM National
1st Floor, Chapel House
18 Hatton Place
London ECIN 8ND
Tel (071) 405 2923

BAC (British Association for
Counselling)
1 Regent Place, Rugby 2PJ
Tel 0788 578328

Bristol Drugs Project
18 Guinea Street
Redcliffe, Bristol BS1 65X
Tel 0272 298047

Community Drug Project
30 Manor Place
London SE17 3BB
Tel 071 7030559

Drug Concern (Harrow)
44 Bessborough Road
Harrow, Middlesex HA1 3DJ
Tel 081 864 9622

Druglink, Trefoil House
Red Lion Lane, Hemel Hempstead
Hertfordshire HP3 9TE
Tel 0923 260733

Families Anonymous
650 Holloway Road
London N19 3NV
Tel (071) 281 8889

ISDD, (Institute for the Study
of Drug Dependence)
Waterbridge House
32-36 Loman Street, London SE1 0EE
Tel (071) 928 1211
Fax (071) 928 1771

Kaleidoscope Youth
and Community Project
40-46 Cromwell Road
Kingston-upon-Thames
Surrey KT2 6RE
Tel 081 549 2681/7488

Milestones
East Lodge
Bexley Hospital
1 Old Bexley Lane, Bexley
Kent DA5 2BW
Tel 0322 5559058

Narcotics Anonymous
UK Service Office
PO Box 198J
London N19 3LS
Helpline (071) 351 6794
Recorded meeting list
281 9933
Publications (071) 272 9040

National AIDS Trust
6th Floor
Eileen House
80 Newington Causeway
London SE1 6AF
Tel (071) 972 2845
Fax (071) 972 2885

National AIDS Helpline
Tel (0800) 567123

Newham Drug Project
39 Wellington Road
London E62RL
Tel 081 552 7225

NW Surrey Substance Misuse Team
Abraham Cowley Unit
Homewood NHS Trust
Holloway Hill, Lyne
Chertsey
Tel (0932) 872010 Ext 3309

Peterborough Community Drug
Team
City Health Clinic
Wellington Street, Peterborough
Cambridgeshire
Tel (0733) 898383

Phoenix House
Head Office
47-49 Borough High Street
London SE1 1NB
Tel (071) 407 2789

Plymouth Community Drug Service
Nuffield Clinic, Seventrees
Lipson Road
Plymouth PL4 8NQ
Tel 0752 660281

Re-Solv, 30a High Street, Stone
Staffordshire
Tel (0785) 817885
Fax (0785) 813205

Solvent Misuse Project
National Children's Bureau
8 Wakley Street
London EC1V 7QE
Tel (071) 278 9441

Standing Conference on Drug Abuse
Tel (071) 928 9500
Fax (071) 928 3343

Terrence Higgins Trust
52-54 Grays Inn Road
London WCIX 8LT
Helpline: (071) 242 1010
Office (071) 831 0330

The Angel Project
38-44 Liverpool Road
London E6 2RQ

Turning Point
New Loom House
101 Back Church Lane
London E1 1LU
Tel (071) 702 2300

West Suffolk Drug Advisory Service
18 St John Street
Bury St Edmunds
Suffolk IP33 ISJ
Tel (0284) 762377

CHANNEL ISLANDS
Alcohol and Drug Service
Catherine Quirke House
2 Newgate Street, St Helier
Jersey
Tel (0534) 59000 Ext 2297

SCOTLAND
Castle Craig Clinic
West Linton
Pebbleshire EH46 7DH
Tel (0721) 52625

Health Education Board for Scotland
Formerly the Scottish Health
Education Group
Woodburn House, Canaan Lane
Edinburgh EH10 4SG
Tel (031) 447 8044

Scottish AIDS Monitor
PO Box 48, Edinburgh EH1 3SA
Office Tel (031) 557 3885
Helpline (0345) 090966
7.30pm-1am weekdays

Scottish Drugs Forum
5 Oswald Street, Glasgow G1 5QR
Tel (041) 221 1175

Scottish Drugs Forum
(Edinburgh Office)
40 Shandwick Place
Edinborough EH@ 4RT
Tel (031) 220 2584

Scottish Drugs Forum
(Dundee office)
84 Commercial Street, Dundee
Tel (0382) 201016

WALES
Community Drug Team
46 Cowbridge Road East
Canton, Cardiff
Tel (0222) 395877

Drugaid: All Wales Drugline
1 Neville Street, Cardiff CF1 8LP
Tel (0222) 383313

Vale Alcohol and Drug Team
(VADT), 236a Holton Road
Barry CF6 6HS
Tel (0446) 700943

Welsh Committee on Drug Misuse
Secretariat, c/o HSSPIA
Welsh Office
Cathays Park
Cardiff CF1 3NQ
Tel (0222) 823 925